Mental Toughness for Young Athletes

Transform from NO ONE to STARDOM

9 Sureshot Techniques to Increase Resilience, Forge an Invincible Mindset, and Succeed in Any Competitive Sport and Beyond

By RK Publishing

Acknowledgment: The cover has been designed using images from Freepik.com.

CONTENTS

INTRODUCTION

"If you're a true warrior, competition doesn't scare you. It makes you better."

— ANDREW WHITWORTH

It's 1978, and a young sophomore named Michael is revved up to join his high school's varsity basketball team.[1] His family had always nurtured in him a love of sports, of competition. Since childhood, he and his father got close by playing baseball, but later, he would choose to commit to basketball, just like his brother. Regardless, that fighting spirit of an athlete had been lit within him, and he thought he could take on anything.

Upon hearing the results of tryouts, Michael was in for a shock.

He didn't make it to varsity.

Maybe it was his height (at 15 or 16 years old, he had yet to grow to a height that would give him leverage). Or maybe he didn't have the skills. Perhaps he wasn't cut out for this stuff. Maybe he should've just done baseball. Maybe it was just his brother's thing, not his. Was it worth trying out next time? If he didn't have it in him, then that was that.

These are all excuses Michael could have used to deter him. But let's just say that Michael didn't have "it" in him ("it" being the natural talent for basketball). Even if that were the case, he had something else inside of him. Something strong and powerful, a driving force that pushed him not to just compete but also to succeed. Michael liked to win. If he lost, he wasn't a good sport about it. Not at all. He couldn't accept the rejection or the loss, and he had to prove to himself that he wasn't a loser.

Since then, Michael began to show up to school long before the first period for access to the gym. There, he would practice, practice, practice. He shot hoops until he was forced out of the gym for class. He didn't stop until he felt he was ready to storm through the next tryouts.

And when it was time, Michael made it on the team. It was a huge victory.

Unfortunately, Michael was on the bench for most of the time, giving out water bottles and towels and watching during the games. It was another tragic defeat. His effort may have seemed pointless; all that sweat . . . just to get a front seat on the sidelines? Maybe the universe was telling Michael that this sport just wasn't for him.

Perhaps it was giving him a critical lesson.

This lesson taught Michael two things. First, he needed to work harder—not just harder, but he had to keep working, doing more than his best because even if he passed a checkpoint on his way to his goal, the job was not over yet. Don't get comfortable, and don't celebrate until you have reached excellence. Secondly, he learned that failure is a necessity, a test to prove one's true heart as a warrior. If he accepts the failure and gives up, that's when he really has lost. If he picks himself up, dusts himself off, and keeps going, he has what it takes to make it to his goal. In other words, it honed his *resilience*.

If Michael had given up the first, second, third, or even fifteenth time he had failed, he wouldn't have become the 6-time Basketball Championship winner, 5-time NBA MVP, and 14-time All-Star player. There would be no Michael Jordan.

Failure is one of the worst feelings in the world, especially if you're a budding athlete. No one wants to sit out at the bench or let their teammates down or come up last place in a competition. But what if we all thought of failure as a test? What if we welcomed it as a lesson that would reveal potential we never knew we had?

It sounds too good to be true, but this is not just about thinking positively.

A mind that sees challenge, competition, and failure as opportunities to improve has honed mental toughness.

In the competitive sporting world, that's what many young athletes need. At this point, it's not the money, training, or skill that will separate the average athlete from the stars. It's the mentality, attitude, and resilience. Without those characteristics, making it far can be difficult. Not only are you trying to beat the odds, but you are also fighting against your own dark, dreary thoughts. Who'll believe in you if you don't?

After all, if you are reading this, you are one of those young athletes who want to make something of yourself. All your life, you've felt a strong connection with your sport; you live it, breathe it. It's impossible to see your future without it. However, as you advance, the world grows bleaker. Coaches and parents may be breathing down your neck. Making mistakes feels more high stakes. Highly skilled athletes in your field are increasingly raising the bar. At this point, it seems like the only way to be one of them is to somehow unlock superpowers or get a radioactive spider bite.

On top of everything, the dominant messages around you aren't helping. Maybe other people keep telling you you're not going to cut it, that you should dream smaller. Maybe you're bogged down by self-doubt. You think you don't have it in you to reach the success you wanted as a child. It's overwhelming, stressful, and frustrating, but most of all, you don't want to let yourself down.

Above all, you have a deep desire, one that feels too big to be possible or too embarrassing to tell others. You want to have a special athletic power no one else has, to be the best in your desired sport, and prove to the world that you are capable of excellence. Your goal is to excel in a sport, make a career out of it, and stand out from the crowd.

Michael's story is not unique to him. He's not the only one to have experienced failing at tryouts or any point in a high school sports career. That's why his story is so great; he was where we all are, and he mastered himself and excelled at his sport. In a way, he is proof that anyone *can* do it, especially if we take notes from his mindset and attitude.

The most important note to jot down? Develop *mental resilience.*

An athlete's mental health strongly affects his or her performance.[2] If there's anything that will allow you to push your limits, it's not working harder, better, or stronger. It's honing your mental resilience, becoming mentally tough to the point where you push yourself past what you thought you were capable of. Without it, there's no drive, discipline, or persistence.

This book can help you master mental resilience by targeting it from all angles. In every chapter, you will learn a valuable, practical technique that you can implement immediately.

It's hard to want to be the best, to thrive in a competitive world, and to find the right resources with correct information in this complex world of available info. You haven't been the only one. Before the understanding that mental resilience is the key, countless athletes struggled to learn this key the hard way. Luckily, this book packages research-based advice, plus the habits and mindsets of famous athletes, into a simple, condensed format with practical how-tos you can apply to your life easily.

After understanding the power of mental resilience and how to use it, you will gain the capacity to push yourself further. You will feel like you are making progress. Moreover, it will help you face whatever life brings with calm and peace, be it a loss or a win. You failed? Get back up and get back to the training ground. What are you doing right? What could you do better? And if you win? Congratulations, keep it up. Don't get complacent. The journey isn't over. There's so much more to do.

This is the mentality that will drive you to success.

1

THE ATHLETIC DREAM

"Our greatest glory is not in never falling, but in rising every time we fall."

— CONFUCIUS

L iving the sports dream: it's something everyone wants. But what does that actually mean for you?

Let's start at the beginning. Sports has always been a dominant part of culture and society, reaching its glorified height in the time of the ancient Greeks. From childhood through adulthood, physical exercise was a necessary part of development into manhood. They would train with activities like running, horse riding, wrestling, javelin throwing, and other exercises fit for a warrior. It wasn't just about preparing for battle, though–physical strength and prowess had an essential place in culture. Ancient cities were littered with free-to-use gymnasiums and palaestra (small gyms for fighting and wrestling). Not to mention, they would spend their time showcasing feats of physical ability in competitions or games.

A BRIEF HISTORY OF SPORT

The Greeks had a lot to say about athleticism and the glory of competing in sports. One could say our current culture around sports is derived from the Greeks.[3] For one, many sports-related terminologies in the English language stem from Greek words. The word gymnast comes from the Greek word *gymnast*, which means trainer. The word athlete comes from *athlos*, which refers to a prize. The word gym comes from *gymnos*, a term that means 'nude' and refers to the fact that ancient Greek men participated in sports absolutely naked. They didn't have tracksuits or sweatpants back then, nor would they have wanted to. Ancient Greek culture, art, and philosophy glorified and admired the muscular male physique. It was a symbol of masculinity and heroism, and watching muscles rippling in action during sports competitions was one of its highlights.

For another, one of the world's most remarkable athletic feat and prowess competitions, the Olympics, comes directly from Greek creation. The Ancient Greeks devised the

Olympics to honor the gods, namely Zeus, the King of the Olympians. They viewed athletics as an opportunity to prove their worth as heroes deserving of the gods' validation, even off the battlefield. The athlete was a hero.

Today, many of us also see athletes as heroes. The world-class champions and winners are the new-age warriors, symbols of ultimate human excellence.

Even for the rest of the relatively average population, be it those who only watch sports or occasionally dabble in sports as physical activity, sports represent something essential to life. Why is it so important to us?

The answer is evident in the fabric of our DNA. Movement is a critical part of being human. The ability to run, jump, climb, and play doesn't and shouldn't stop at the end of childhood. Back when humans were cave dwellers, hunters, and gatherers, physical strength and agility were necessary for survival. The strongest, fastest of us were the survivors. In honoring the evolutionary pattern of survival of the fittest, those who lived to pass on their genes would contribute to a line of more strong and fast survivors. Evolutionarily, athletic prowess meant the continuation of the human race.

Luckily, these rules no longer bind us today.

In the modern world, those skills are no longer necessary. We don't need to chase animals for our next meal or stand out in the sun for twelve hours a day, toiling to subsist on the grains of the earth to feed our community. We don't need immense physical strength to protect our families, communities, or tribes, yet we respect and admire those abilities. Since they are no longer necessary, we see them as a notable example of human discipline and pure work ethic to see an athlete perform them.

In lieu of the need for athleticism to fight in battles or protect one's home, competitive sport has become a popular pastime. Otherwise, for what would humans use their amazing potential?

The saying, "If you don't use it, you lose it," rings true when it comes to human potential. Sports give us an exciting mentally and physically stimulating way to discover what we or our rivals are made of. Eventually, competitive sports became a somewhat friendlier way for people and nations to compete and measure each other's strengths.

THE SOCIO-EMOTIONAL ROLE OF SPORTS

Besides its clear physical benefits, the culture around sports has a meaningful impact on society and the individual.

From historical civilizations came the birth of sport as an enjoyable activity without the purpose of defending, fighting, or surviving. Ancient Egyptians enjoyed wrestling, archery, and swimming. Roman gladiators fought to the death in the Colosseum as pure public entertainment. The European Medieval ages birthed games like jousting and an early form of soccer (football), as well as wrestling and hunting. The 19th century would give rise to the modern version of soccer we know today, as well as tennis, cricket, softball, ice hockey, horse racing, and more.[4]

The world of modern sports represents the healthy competition between two teams or rivals. It also represents classical values that may have been lost somewhere along the line. Values like hope, honor, fairness, victory, and respect are kept alive by sporting events.[5]

Groups of people from all walks of life may gather together to cheer on their team, creating a sense of connection that we seldom feel in today's highly independent world. It creates a sense of collectivity, of national or local identity. Sports fans can enjoy a good conversation, no matter how different they are, regardless of gender, race, or status. Holding sporting events is also a way to boost a city or country's economic state, helping with tourism and local businesses.

For competitors, engaging in sports can spur their feeling of belonging in a team or a place in the world. It can give them a sense of purpose, a heightened self-confidence. Sports offer a healthy way to regulate emotions when played regularly or even casually. It's a way to escape the stress of life and add excitement for both players and onlookers.

Sports have had the power to pause war and create truces. The soccer World Cup, for example, has created temporary peace more than once. On one Christmas Eve of 1914, during World War I, soldiers on opposing sides met in the middle of no man's land to play a game of soccer.[6] While brief, the game made friends of enemies and peace of war. It's just one of many instances in which sports have had the power to connect people on opposing sides.

It can also be a way to promote awareness of social problems. In the 1936 Olympics in Berlin, Germany, Adolf Hitler intended to make the event a way to spread his propaganda of Aryan athletic superiority over other races. To his dismay, African-American sprinter Jesse Owens won four gold medals and would go on to break many records. The sports world is where even racial disparities and discrimination become meaningless in the face of victory.

SPORTS FOR A HEALTHY LIFESTYLE

Let's not forget the obvious benefits of sports and other types of athletics. It can be a part of a healthy lifestyle without making physical activity feel tiring or tedious. The exhilaration of sports training, especially when you have to meet a goal or standard, can challenge you and push you to a limit you never thought you could surpass.

As long as there's a healthy balance between your sport and other facets of life, physical activity provides stress relief and boosts brain health. It's an ideal way to release negative emotions. Not to mention the immense benefits of sleep quality—something we could all use.

As a young athlete, of course, you're not interested in sports as a casual addition to your daily routine. Your specific sport actually takes up a huge chunk of your time; you are aiming for a life dedicated to it.

SPORTS AS A CAREER

Sports offer a way to prove you are capable of immense success because you can see the physical progress of your hard work and dedication.

In this fast-paced world where many sports champions cross lines and beat records, what does it mean to be an accomplished athlete? What does success truly mean? Can any average boxer try to be the next Muhammad Ali or Mike Tyson? Can a budding basketball player in high school aim to join the ranks of Michael Jordan or Kobe Bryant? The meaning of a successful sports career varies from person to person.

For many children and teens rising to the ranks of their sport, an adult might give the definition of success—like a parent or a coach. Young athletes can feel a lot of pressure on their end, and their sport of choice becomes less enjoyable. By their late teens, it feels like a job, with overwhelming pressure bombarding from all sides.[7]

While success is a worthy goal, it's not worth losing what made the sport fun in the first place. Too much pressure and focus on results can actually reduce confidence and affect performance. You don't want to have to force yourself to get up every morning to train; you want to *enjoy* the process.

The important thing is to clear away the noise and choose the right goal for you, one that is rooted in your values. This can be hard since you have a lot of resistance to go up against. Coaches, parents, and peers might spark doubt about your purpose. However, that's what mental toughness is for. It's not just having the willpower to get up and do what you don't like. It's also to stand up for what you think is right in terms of your sports career. It's time to start steering the course that would most fulfill you to excel.

After all, excelling in sports today is complicated on such a competitive playing field. There are many contenders world-wide reaching for the champion title. To be great, you must really surpass modern expectations. Achieving your goal, whether you want to be great locally or internationally, will be difficult.

With that in mind, you need more skills at your disposal. Athleticism requires more than just physical strength or knowing the rules, techniques, and tricks of a sport. A strong body and an enduring body require a *resilient mind*. To stand out today, you must nurture a mind that is resilient enough to believe in and achieve your goal.

Without your mind in the right place, your body will not get you where you want to be. That's another reason why we admire many celebrity athletes, not just for their never-before-seen basket dunk or record-breaking speed but also because we are in awe of their dedication to reaching a level of unimaginable skill. They inspire us with their unstoppable hard work and persistence. We know that if we could just unlock that kind of mental control, we could be like them too.

Resilience. Mental fortitude. Unbreakable resolve.

Always get back up. Never give up.

These age-old adages seem cliché and self-evident. Yet, if we really were to reach our breaking point, would we keep going or give up? How easy would it be to keep trying after the first five, twenty, or even fifty tries end in failure? Most of us struggle to keep going after failure. However, it's true that agility, strength, and ability don't work in isolation. The body must work in tandem with the mind, the heart, and the soul to push yourself to the next level.

THE SPIRIT OF SPORT

Spirit is absolutely tied with sports. Athletics can help hone that resilience, especially if you have the attitude that every time you fail is an opportunity to improve. In sports psychology, it's clear that sports and athletics contribute to a strong spirit, a positive mindset, and an unshakeable character.

Sports can provide many advantages in developing your character:

- Learn selflessness in teamwork
- Respect fairness and others
- Embody a competitive spirit that also respects your opponent's skill
- Cultivate an intense focus on the present
- Feel glory even in defeat
- Learn to value the process more than the outcome
- Develop planning skills
- Nurture a habit of executing action
- Adaptation during unexpected setbacks
- Manage fear and anxiety

All of these skills are essential outside of the training gym or the field. That's why so many famous athletes are inspirational to us because, on their way to the top, they had to hone their spirit and attitude to keep going. You may want to maximize your ability in your sport and achieve these elements. However, this requires having a solid direction in life. You might have a powerful drive to build a sustainable sports career. This starts with getting clear on who you are and what you want: the first step to developing mental toughness.

2

PICK YOUR DIRECTION

"Efforts and courage are not enough without purpose and direction."

— JOHN F. KENNEDY

For many, the issue is not a lack of hard work but a lack of direction. Often, our dreams are vague and intangible. That makes it hard to strategize or even believe we can accomplish them. To tackle this issue, you must know who you are and what you want in life in relation to your athletic goal. This is the key to excellence in sports.

If you're an athlete, your sport is incredibly important to who you are. It might even be a major part of your identity. Of course, this comes with a lot of advantages. Athletic identity is tied to positive effects on one's involvement, connection, and performance within the sport.[8] At the same time, your identity might not be enough to drive you to where you think you want to go. However, you can always use your identity as a starting point to choose the direction you want to head toward.

SURESHOT TECHNIQUE #1: HAVE A CLEAR DIRECTION IN LIFE

Discover who you are and where you want to go. If you don't know, you will never get "there" because you don't know where "there" is.

Many young athletes don't get a chance to choose what they want for themselves. They often absorb what the world around them says they need to reach for. If they never connect to that goal, they may run out of steam. The way to choose a long-term direction is to be authentic to yourself. That way, the goal is so strongly a part of you that it will push you beyond the edges of the earth.

Make Authentic Value-Based Goals

Mara Abbott, cycling champion of the 2016 Olympics, used the power of authentic goals to drive her beyond winning a sports event.[9] Abbott left the sport due to a conflict with her purpose. While she loved cycling, she was also an environmentalist at heart. Being a cyclist for a living didn't seem to have any special place, except for using up plastic water bottles for hydration. Abbot quietly left the biking scene in 2011.

She thought long and hard about what dent she wanted to make in the world. What did cycling mean to her? What did she desire cycling to mean to her?

Eventually, Abbot made a comeback at the 2013 Giro Rosa after revitalizing her passion, but this time for a new goal. In her own words: "I wanted desperately to see just how good I could be if I committed. My primary motivation became devoting myself to the abstract value of living out my full potential."

Certain goals spark something inside you. They have filled you with awe and hunger since a young age. Somewhere along the way, you were forced to be realistic, reign in your dream, and pick a practical goal, like winning a specific contest or passing a doable record. However, Abbott says that it's those huge, insane-sounding goals that will keep you going forever. They will make you enjoy every part of the process, making you train hard for the sake of it.

Another reason to determine your own goal is because you can't go into your sports career always following the opinions of others; that can lead to burnout. At some point, you need to be honest with yourself about why you are doing this. What are you willing to do to get there? How will you keep yourself in line without a coach, a team, or the crowds?

Sometimes an authentic goal will sound more like a movie character's aim. Maybe you want to be like Muhammad Ali, whose goal was to be the greatest. Perhaps you want to live to your fullest potential, like cyclist Mara Abbott, who wanted to fulfill her potential in life. Say you want to be the strongest person in the world or be remembered forever. Both of these are lofty goals. It doesn't matter how unrealistic the goal sounds as long as it is a key part of your values. The bigger the goal, the longer the fuel will drive you.

As athletes, it can be easy to absorb societal ideals. Coaches, parents, and the community around you may push you in a certain direction. However, this direction might not resonate with who you are. That's why it's essential to consider your identity when choosing your authentic goal.

THE IMPORTANCE OF IDENTITY

Identity is who you believe yourself to be. It can bring comfort and resolution when it comes to life's challenges. When we know who we are, we have confidence in our strengths and have a foundation to be mentally tough individuals. It's what keeps us unique and sets us apart from others. In sports, this is what brings us gold. Winning is just as much about your story of who you are as it is about your practice or performance. Identity empowers individuals to chase after their goals, stay true to themselves, and have trust in their choices.[10]

How do you have an authentic goal if you don't know who you are?

Environment, family, culture, society, and many other factors contribute to identity. As you grow older, you start to think about your place in life and how you relate to the world around you. You might embody new roles and leave others. Identity exploration is a normal part of life, no matter your age. Sometimes you might not know who you are or how your sport fits into your life. As young adults, your identity is not yet set in stone. In fact, it might never have to be.[11] You can choose who you want to develop into rather than let your life continue with whatever trajectory it is going. It's not just about discovering your sense of self but about growing into your ideal self.

In this case, think of yourself as a project rather than focusing on being yourself. Continuously reinvent yourself, try new opportunities, test new perspectives, and get out of your comfort zone. Challenging your brain with new, fresh ideas and activities will create new neurological connections on a biological level and mentally help you strengthen your character.

Discover Who You Really Are

If you're not yet happy with who you are, it's important to reflect every once in a while. Think about what traits you identify with. Are they helpful or not helpful to you when it comes to your goal (authentic or not)? You have the power to explore what you accept as your identity.

Constructing your identity will look like this: some effort, some discipline, and a whole lot of discovery. To get clear on your direction in life, gain more information on your likes, dislikes, values, boundaries, strengths, and weaknesses. The following tips will help you do this:

Know Your Likes and Dislikes

Truly acknowledging what you like and do not like increases self-awareness.[12] It helps you feel connected to or stand apart from others. The things you like or dislike are clues. They show you what you might enjoy doing in life. They reveal your strengths and weaknesses. More practically, they can guide you to a career path, hobby, or skill you might not have considered. Sometimes, it can even tell you if you have been too constrictive on yourself by focusing on one thing over another.

Know Your Values

Values are your beliefs about what is most crucial in everything you do.[13] Whether you know your values or not, what is important to you will show through your actions, choices, and feelings. If something feels forced or wrong, it probably doesn't align with your values.

Sometimes your values might be there, but they may not be clear enough for you to act deliberately on them. This can lead to conflicting priorities in life. To choose your direction, know your values. That way, you have a strong motivating force inside you.

Reflect on moments of satisfaction, pride, or contentment to uncover your values. What times during training make you feel the most content? Or with family? Or at school? When were you most proud of yourself, and why? When did you feel your needs or desires in life and sports were fulfilled? When you worked hard on a skill and finally accomplished it after months of grueling work? Try to narrow down the factors that contributed to these feelings because they will clue you into your values. These will show you your values.[14]

Many career athletes value achievement, ambition, excellence, and competitiveness. Others involved in sports like ice skating or gymnastics might value precision, discipline, and elegance.

In fact, if you think about your athletic life so far and what moments made you feel more fulfilled, it may reveal values that can guide you through life outside of sports. Knowing this information will allow you to make value-based decisions without caring as much about external influences.

Set Boundaries

By knowing your values, principles, and beliefs, you can determine what matters in life and what boundaries you want to set between yourself and others. If you value integrity, you will not accept maintaining a friendship with someone prone to cheating. Boundaries are the limits we set, not only for ourselves but also for our relationships. By setting your boundaries, you are ensuring you surround yourself with people who will not lead you off the path you want to follow.

Boundaries are also about prioritizing your needs. Take care of your health and well-being so that you have more of yourself to give energy to training, performance, game, and other areas (social, family, work, school, etc.).

To figure out boundaries, try spending some time on your own.[15] You must get to know yourself better and gain clarity on what you are or are not comfortable with.

DISCOVER YOUR STRENGTHS AND WEAKNESSES

When considering your direction, focus on your strengths and support your weaknesses.[16]

Create a List of All the Strengths You Know[17]

A strength is not just something you're good at but something that gives you energy and inspires you. True strength is a combination of what comes easily to you, fuels you, and is enjoyable. Maybe you've found that your strength lies in providing outstanding leadership—that this motivates you to be a better team leader and invigorates you throughout the game. Perhaps you've found strength in assisting your team-mates, continuously pushing you to be a better player. What-ever your strength is, make a list of anything that really inspires you and continually motivates you in your game.

Consider Hidden Strengths You Don't Yet Know

Ask people if they see any strengths in you that you haven't yet realized. Others will be able to see strengths you might be overlooking. Your friends, teammates, and family members will see a side of you that you've never considered before and bring more awareness to your strengths. The next step is to think about how you can better use your strengths to their fullest potential.

Write a List of Anything You Struggle With

Weaknesses will overlap with some of the things you hate doing. While it's best to focus on your strengths, weaknesses can also be a potential point of importance.[18] However, this is only if the benefits of overcoming or improving your weakness outweigh the costs. In other words, if a weakness would be valuable to improve, both for your sport or your life, then do so.

Some Ways to Turn a Weakness Into a Strength:

- Change the question from "Why can't I do this?" to "How can I do this despite the challenge?"
- Consider if the weakness comes from limiting beliefs or a skill-based issue.

GET CLEAR ON WHAT YOU WANT

To get more clarity on what you want, there are a few easy things to do:

Take 'Should' Out of Your Vocabulary

First, throw out the word "should" from your vocabulary.[19] Saying, "I should train," or "I should be able to do this," or "I shouldn't do that" is not true to yourself. It's based on the sense of what you think society would approve of or disapprove of. More importantly, it has nothing to do with your true goal. Instead, change your vocabulary to something more concrete. Instead of "should," tell yourself "will"; I *will* train today, I *will* do this. The way you speak to yourself will help strengthen your mentality and create a more positive mindset.

Think Critically About Outside Opinions

Remember to think critically about what other people tell you. It can be easy to feel like you don't know much and that you are better off listening to the judgments and opinions of others because they probably know more.

While it's valuable to consider the advice of people with more experience and knowledge, the key is not to blindly accept any opinion.

Here's a rule of thumb: take what is helpful and leave what doesn't apply to you. Or, if a person is not living the life you dream of, maybe take their words with a grain of salt. Everyone is more self-serving than they might seem. Separate other people's agendas from what is true, authentic, and aligns with your values.[20] It's your life, not theirs.

Get in Touch With Your Body's Signals

Finally, get in touch with your body to know what a *yes* or *no* feels like.[21] Athletes are very physical people who know more about their physiological and anatomical abilities than anyone. Yet it can be hard to focus on what your gut instinct is telling you. Get used to listening to it. If an activity sparks excitement in you, that's a *yes*. If someone offering you an opportunity ignites dread or unease, that's a *no*.[22]

VISUALIZE SUCCESS IN YOUR GOALS EVERY DAY

Focusing on a certain trajectory in your life requires a strong mind-body connection. One way to keep going in the right direction is to use the power of visualization.

One man stuck in a bleak situation had only his mind and nothing else to keep him sane. In the 1970s, Natan Sharansky was imprisoned in a dreadful Siberian jail by the Russian government, assumed to be an American spy.

He was stuck in prison for 12 years in a tiny, cramped cell with nothing to do and no one to talk to. It was just him and his mind. Sharansky coped by keeping himself occupied with chess. *Mental* chess.[23]

Yes, he played chess in his mind. He began visualizing the chess board and making moves against an imaginary opponent. As you can imagine, it took a lot of work to picture something purely from memory. Still, Sharansky kept it up until the chess board and individual pieces were clearly vivid in his mind. He calculated his responses to countless possible moves. Eventually, he imagined a worthy opponent to play against—the world champion at that time, Gary Kasparov.

Twelve years passed, and Sharansky was finally released under Bill Clinton's presidency. He returned to Israel. One fateful day, Gary Kasparov was visiting Israel for a chess event. Sharansky was also there and one of Kasparov's five opponents. By the end, he was the only one to beat Kasparov.

It was all through the power of will and visualization.[23] By the time Sharansky had faced the real thing, it felt like brushing his teeth or taking a walk; it was automatic.

Training doesn't always have to be hard work. You can use the power of your imagination to get some practice in—literally. For instance, you might visualize yourself performing your training regime, especially the most challenging aspects you can never seem to overcome. Or, you might visualize your desired daily routine that will take you to success, playing it in your mind every night like a movie. Or perhaps you even visualize the very end: the positive outcome of your efforts.

According to a study, the same brain patterns activated when lifting weights in the gym were triggered when the weightlifters visualized themselves lifting.[24] Many athletes use this technique to not only hone their skills but also conceptualize facing any unexpected moves, like preparing for anything in a chess match. Tiger Woods and Muhammad Ali have used this technique to boost their performance. If anything, visualization increases belief in yourself.

If mentally envisioning something vividly is hard for you, don't worry. The first few times will be fuzzy, but you will improve with practice. One trick to try is this: before you try something, like throwing a ball into a hoop, close your eyes for a few seconds and have that image in front of you. See yourself making the shot. Then, open your eyes and let them free. Over time, visualization and other mental exercises can improve the connection between your cognition and your body.

Whatever you do, make sure you attach a positive emotion, like relief, joy, pride, happiness, and the thrill of victory, to your visualization.

Try this: Put your self-reflection into motion by trying the following tips:

START JOURNALING EVERY DAY TO REVEAL AND REFLECT ON WHO YOU ARE

Journaling is a key mental-health-boosting tool.[25] It's like a DIY therapy session where you can unload your anxieties, reconsider negative thoughts and cope with the stress of each day.

Benefits of Journaling Consistently

- **Self-knowledge:** Journaling lets you learn more about yourself and what you really want in life. Knowing yourself is the best power you can have. Self-knowledge unlocks a grounded foundation that helps you stand your ground even when other peoples' opinions threaten to sway you.
- **Fuel your goal:** Use your journal to remind yourself of your main purpose or goal. Life can often distract us from what's important, but journaling provides a way to instill that passion for our goal daily. Make your goal so high a priority that you become obsessed with doing whatever it takes to reach it.
- **Make better decisions:** Working through your thought process on paper helps you come to a clear, logical decision.

Starting your journal is easy: just use any notebook, as simple or as fancy as you'd like, and start writing daily. Add it to your routine, morning or evening, and don't filter your thoughts.

Create a Success Journal

Being humble is great but cranking up the volume on what you're good at could differentiate you from other athletes. Starting now, write down *three things* you accomplished every day, even if it's as small as waking up an hour earlier to train or as big as beating your own sprinting record.[26]

Benefits of a Success Journal

- Increase your confidence and self-esteem
- Gain knowledge of your strengths
- Discover hidden strengths you're not aware of
- Narrow down your direction in life by letting your skills and talents guide you

When you polish up your goal and embark on it, you may find some challenges come along the way. Be it external or internal obstacles, you need to uncover what is holding you back and no longer serving you on the path to success.

3

KNOW WHAT BREAKS YOU DOWN

"And every day, the world will drag you by the hand, yelling, "This is important! And this is important! And this is important! You need to worry about this! And this! And this!" And each day, it's up to you to yank your hand back, put it on your heart and say, "No. This is what's important."

— IAIN THOMAS

The first step to building mental toughness is to tackle your Achilles' heel: your weaknesses, the stuff holding you back, and any external or internal blind spots in your life. Without this, you risk leaving yourself open to getting worn out repeatedly. No matter how much effort you put into your athletic goal, you might feel like you're spinning your wheels, and something is keeping you back from performing at your full potential.

The things that break you down weaken you on every level. Here's how you can reduce this in your life:

SURESHOT TECHNIQUE #2: GET CLEAR ON WHAT IS HOLDING YOU BACK

Irish gymnast Keiran Behan was only ten when he had to get surgery for a cancerous tumor on his thigh.[27] He was an up-and-coming gymnast and very promising at his young age. After the operation went south, Behan was forced to be in a wheelchair for fifteen months. The recovery set him back, but even as a kid, he went straight back to the gym afterward.

After several months of trying to get his preoperative gymnastics progress back, Keiran fell into a head injury that led to blackouts, lack of coordination, headaches, and more. He had to miss school, use a walking stick, face bullying, and undergo physical therapy to improve his brain-body connection. Still, he refused to quit his goal of becoming a champion gymnast, even if it took him three years just to return to his initial shape, even if his bones and tendons strained in the process. Eventually, Keiran did become a World Cup champion.

What can we learn from Keiran's story? Even the most damaging, permanent setbacks can be overcome, no matter what doctors, loved ones, classmates, or others say. No matter how many times Keiran was physically held back by injuries, he still had a childhood dream he wanted to achieve. Instead of saying, "What if I ruin my body?" he sought the best ways to recover his body after every fall and even overcame the prospect of training hard to get back to his initial state of fitness. This is what it means to embody the spirit of a resilient athlete.

It is also what it looks like to know what breaks you down, mentally and physically. Keiran's example shows us that in every setback he experienced, he took it not as an opportunity to quit but as a problem to solve.

Often, many people (not just athletes) see an obstacle as a reason to stop. Of course, obstacles, weaknesses, and problems are painful. Owing to that pain, we instinctively try to avoid the situation by giving up. After all, if a problem stops you from playing your sport, then stopping that sport will make that problem irrelevant.

However, if we face the problem instead of giving up, we can see it more clearly. Then, we can look for the right solutions.

This is what Keiran did. What he went through was so emotionally draining that he could have easily walked away from gymnastics a long time ago. The things that most of us face may not be as severe as Keiran's, but any hardship can destroy our morale, motivation, and determination to keep going.

What if we could embody Keiran's spirit? If we could get to know our weak spots rather than pretend they don't exist, it would open up a huge well of opportunity. It creates long-term fuel for overcoming obstacles and staying on your path to the goal.

We do this by figuring out what holds you back. That said, here are some common things that can break anyone down:

1. Too much complexity
2. Poor emotional regulation
3. Ignoring basic needs

Identify which obstacles are specific to you and tackle them with a vengeance.

OBSTACLE 1: TOO MUCH COMPLEXITY

Complexity is a double-edged sword. At its worst, it's bad news for both the brain and the soul.[29] There's only so much attention but an incredible amount of information to store, think about, consider, and remember. At any given time, you can only hold so much information in your memory. Having too much on your mind can prevent you from focusing and staying on course. You may need to prioritize things to keep your mind clear.

Things should be as simple as possible.

How do you simplify your life?[30] There are a few things you can do:

1. Drop, defer, delegate
2. Cut out self-defeating habits
3. Stop mental chatter
4. Work on time management
5. Be mindful of your choices

Most of the time, you don't need all of that complexity. You will find the more you cut out, the more at peace you are, and the better you can concentrate on what's important and pour your time and energy into your top obligations and goals. You can better identify opportunities and solutions when you cut through the world's noise.

Simplifying complexity is essential in both physical and mental areas. As an athlete, you want to optimize your environment to give you the best chance at success. That means keeping your home or bedroom clean, your things organized, and your clutter out of sight. A neat and clean environment gives you peace of mind.

Drop, Defer, and Delegate

Let's face it: not everything you do in your daily life will help push you to be the best version of yourself. Sometimes, we think that in order to be the best or the greatest, we have to do every little task that's asked of us. But that simply isn't true. Sometimes, you just have to say "no" and learn to let others help you when necessary.

No matter where you're at in life, take inventory of what you do and learn to say *no* to the things that don't serve you. Or, simply delegate it to others and consider it a lower priority. This principle is used by successful people in business but can work for anyone, including athletes.

For example, if you're focused on an upcoming competition, you will have to defer or hold off on any new opportunities for later sports events. If your schedule is always packed, you may want to start saying no to activities or engagements so you can reserve some time for rest, relaxation, and contemplation.

Cut Out Self-Defeating Habits

Simplifying complexity also means cutting out the unnecessary things in your life, namely those in your control. Some of these things include certain habits you may engage in that feel normal but might actually be holding you back.

For instance, overthinking is a common habit that can not only increase the complexity of a situation but also bog you down, leading to time wasted. It can feel like you're going one step forward and two backward. Unhealthy mental patterns fill up your mind with useless thoughts and chatter. It may even show up as negative self-talk and lead to low feelings that deter you from staying determined.

To cut out self-defeating habits, try these steps . . .[31]

1. The first step to cutting out self-defeating habits is to be aware of your actions. Start by paying attention to how you think and behave now. The better you are at being aware of yourself, the sooner you can catch yourself before engaging in maladaptive habits.

2. Consistent, long-term work starts with a decision. It's crucial that, if you want to reduce self-defeating habits, you make a commitment to changing your life.

3. Most self-defeating habits start with negative thoughts. Aim to nurture a positive mindset by saying supportive mantras and affirmations daily or interrupting the negative stream of thoughts with rational and balanced thoughts.

4. Focus on your goals and make this change in self-defeating habits a part of it. Connecting your habit change to the bigger picture puts it into perspective and increases motivation to stick to your change.

5. Remember that improvement is what counts. Even if you improve by just 1% daily, that's worth a lot. Research shows that focusing on improvement-based rather than mastery goals increases your positive attitude, making you more likely to stick to your habit change.[32]

Like any other habit, self-defeating habits need alternatives. Replace those habits with healthier habits. Try focusing on your most concerning self-defeating habits. For example, you might counteract overthinking with meditation, positive self-talk, and journaling.

Manage Your Time

Finally, reduce complexity by mastering your time. An athlete's time is their greatest asset. Yet, it's easy to fall into mindless behaviors or activities that may waste your time. If you want to achieve your big dream, you don't have time to waste. Simplify your schedule and prioritize the activities that will contribute to your goal. If you master your time, the time you spend on things will be reduced from weeks to days and days to hours.

Be Mindful of Your Choices

At the end of the day, make a habit of examining every act you do or choice you make. Ask yourself, *"Is it bringing me closer to my goal or not?"*

If you're unsure whether a habit is bringing you down or not, you need to reflect. For example, some athletes might think that being overly critical and self-punishing in their minds will push them to do better. In reality, this is more likely to break you down.

OBSTACLE 2: LACK OF EMOTIONAL SELF-REGULATION

Controlling emotions is a huge part of gaining mental toughness. However, many people are not in tune with their emotions. This means they may be unable to manage them, especially at the moment.

Most people behave out of fear rather than love. In other words, they are operating in automatic mode: not deliberate, conscious actions. You might be one of these people too. After all, learning and developing emotional self-regulation is a life-long journey.

In this case, two possible factors may be holding you back:

1. People around you are reacting on impulse out of negative emotions
2. You are unable to keep fear from driving your actions

To manage what could break you down emotionally, you'll need to learn how to:

- Manage your emotions and reactions
- Deal with energy vampires
- Set up healthy boundaries
- Prevent toxic people from getting you down
- Grow your self-awareness

Manage Your Emotions and Reactions

Start with what is directly in your control by learning to regulate your emotions. Learning to let go of fear, or more specifically, overcome it, is a key skill you can hone.[33] Fear can lead to avoidance of what you need to do, a feeling of being paralyzed, and overwhelming feelings of anxiety.

In the professional landscape of sports, fear can immobilize you, keeping you from performing your best. Whether you are afraid of failure or afraid of reaching out for an opportunity, managing your fear is essential.

You can do a few things to let go of fear, many backed by research and others by ancient stoic thinkers.[34]

1. First, take note of all your fears. Take a piece of paper and jot down everything that sends your heart speeding or your stomach churning in anxiety.
2. Once you have your list down, circle the ones most likely to keep you from your goal, namely your athletic vision.
3. Now, you must tackle them. Yes, the only way to overcome fear is through it: facing it on your own terms. Make a decision to gradually become comfortable feeling this fear and doing it anyway.
4. For each of your top fears, visualize what you can do to tackle them when they occur.
5. Then, make a plan to continue performing despite each fear.

For instance, if you are a gymnast and you fear slipping in front of a crowd, prioritize that fear. Make a plan for everything you can do to prepare for that outcome. Maybe you'll train harder. Maybe you'll practice protective techniques to prevent yourself from losing your grip. Document all possible weak points that could lead to the outcome. Then, execute the plan. Sharpen your skills to shield yourself from the outcome that terrifies you.

Another way to take action is to simply visualize yourself falling and practice feeling okay with that outcome. This is called *negative visualization* and has been shown to increase people's acceptance and reduce disappointment's destructive effects.[35] Becoming familiar with the worst-case scenario will aid you in becoming mentally and emotionally prepared for anything. The fear of things going wrong is much worse than them going wrong. It's much better to fall in front of a crowd a dozen times than risk your fear freezing you.

There are plenty of practical techniques to use amid a fear-wracking moment. *Controlling your breath* is one of them. Deep breathing and keeping your inhales and exhales steady, even as your heart beats out of control, can regulate your nervous system. More importantly, it helps you feel more in control of the situation. Even if you have little say in the final outcome, you still have control over your breath, your mind, and your body.

Mentally, use *positive visualization* in those high-stakes moments to keep you calm and centered. Have a go-to image or place in your mind that immediately fills you with peace, whether it's imagining yourself with a gold medal or surrounded by family at the holiday dinner table.

People around you may bring you down with their fears and negative reactions. Energy vampires are people who suck the energy (not blood) out of you. Maybe spending time with them leaves you feeling drained. More than that, they may act manipulatively. They may be self-centered. Whether they are aware of their behavior or not, energy vampires can cause a lot of stress for you.[33]

To avoid the grasp of the energy vampires, try these tips recommended by Christiane Northrup, MD, author of *Dodging Energy Vampires:*[36]

- **Grey rock them:** Grey rocking refers to the act of not responding the way an energy vampire wants. Be short, boring, and uninterested. Often, they'll be put off by the new behavior, but only because you're not giving them attention. If they wonder why you changed, just say you're tired. With time, they will lose interest.
- **Maintain cool indifference:** Never overreact or show too much emotion around an energy vampire. They love to feed on emotions and use them to fuel their outbursts. Instead, staying calm and indifferent will throw them off.

- **Learn to say 'no':** Don't be afraid to say *no* to the energy vampire, even if they are unhappy. If they make you feel guilty, you'll know the truth . . . they don't mean well.
- **Cut them out of your life:** If someone is more draining than energizing, consider cutting them out. If the relationship is not healthy or mutually beneficial but rather affecting your life and even your sport, it's time to end things.
- **Know when to leave:** Offering sympathy to someone who is venting is fine. But when the conversation is heavily focused on the energy vampires' problems, it's time to exit. You'll know if it's time when the energy vampire complains, no matter how many solutions you offer.

Whether the people around you are energy vampires or not, having boundaries is critical at all times.

Set Up Healthy Boundaries

Boundaries are the lines between your and other people's physical and emotional space.[37] But it's not just a self-created wall; it's also a way of respecting your needs and desires in any interaction with another person. In other words, you manage and balance your needs with the needs of others.

What does it mean to have unhealthy boundaries exactly? It can mean not having any boundaries at all. It may mean that you haven't solidly and consistently defined them or aren't actively enforcing your boundaries. A dynamic relationship with unhealthy boundaries is when two people in a relationship, be it professional, friendly, or familiar, have an imbalance in fulfilling needs. For instance, one person might be more vocal and pushier about what they require, while the other is more agreeable and keeps their needs repressed. It also looks like feeling responsible for things you can't control. No matter how it manifests, unhealthy boundaries are exactly that: unhealthy. Over time, they can weigh down a person's well-being.

Mental toughness is not about being able to handle anything that comes your way with strength and resolve. It's actually about being in control of your time and energy in relation to other people and gaining the assertiveness to uphold your boundaries. If your friends are pressuring you to go out frequently, even when you don't feel like it or know you'd rather be practicing your sport, boundaries help you balance your wants and needs alongside others. One example of a boundary is to dedicate weekends to fun and social outings and weekdays for training.

Creating and upholding healthy boundaries reduces emotional dysregulation. You focus on what you value, you respect yourself, and you are only responsible for what you control.

What is in your realm of control? Your thoughts, emotions, attitudes, perspectives, beliefs, speech, and actions. No one else's. Once you think of it this way, you can begin to think critically about what really matters and what doesn't.

However, even if you have a handle on yourself, you will inevitably come across some difficult people. It's good to prepare for dealing with them when the time comes.

How to Avoid Toxic People

Toxic people tend to be self-absorbed, manipulative, and emotionally abusive and may cause problems for those around them. Try to keep an eye out for the following: if they are repeatedly lying to you or gaslighting you, fail to apologize after making a clear mistake, or make you feel like the bad guy even when you logically did nothing wrong. Otherwise, they may dominate the conversation consistently, minimize your experience, or turn everything back to them.

To avoid toxic people, keep your distance, slowly reduce contact, and create some space.[38] For example, you can be polite toward a family member without getting too invested or sharing your weaknesses and vulnerabilities. Set boundaries, mentally and physically. Know that the actions of others are not your responsibility.

To supplement this, know the signs of a person whose behavior positively influences your life: emotionally intelligent, forgiving, and the kind of person who can let things go and move on. If the toxic person was very close to you, it's okay to seek another person's support while you grieve the loss of that relationship.

Grow Your Self-Awareness

Self-awareness is critical not to letting your ego get to you.[39] The ego is the part of you that is vulnerable to criticism, failure, and looking bad. At every moment, your ego tries to lie to you so that you can remain comfortable and protect your self-image. This means you may be blind to your faults or ways that might be blocking you from achieving what you want.

The key is to garner awareness of what you are telling yourself and doing at all times. Mental toughness is not possible without self-awareness. If it were up to your ego, you'd think you're fine as you are, and the world is out to get you! Self-awareness reveals your weaknesses so that you can tackle them right away. To be more self-aware, you need to do a few things:

- Know yourself more
- Sit with yourself in silence
- Take account of your progress
- Seek feedback from friends, peers, or coaches

To *know yourself more*, try journaling.

To be able to *sit with yourself in silence* and separate your ego's chatter from the clarity of your true self, try meditation.

To *take account of your progress*, try tracking your goals and what you're doing each day in your routine to get there.[40] What are your expectations? Are you meeting them? What's working and what's not?

Finally, to *seek feedback*, practice opening yourself up to criticism and take it with honor. Remember that no criticism means you're not improving. How can you when you don't have an objective view of what you're doing wrong? Your perception of your effort and skills differs from what others might see. If you want to train yourself to a point where you can join the ranks of the sporting world, you need to have an honest take on your performance.

OBSTACLE 3: IGNORING BASIC NEEDS

All humans, especially athletes, need to have their basic needs covered to be able to thrive. Those categories include: Physical, Mental, Emotional, Spiritual, and Social.[41]

Physical: Take care of your body consistently. A balanced diet is crucial for an athlete. Fill up on lean proteins, fresh vegetables, fruits, and legumes. Reduce junk food and sugar. You're already doing a lot of physical activity as an athlete, which is great. However, it means you must rest too. Sleeping 7–9 hours a night is non-negotiable for growing athletes, as it improves recovery, health, and performance.

Mental: Taking care of your body will set you up for stable mental health.[42] Yet it's also good to throw in some activities that boost your well-being, like getting enough sun, going out in nature, gratitude journaling, taking regular breaks, and practicing mindfulness. Break up your routine with enjoyable, low-effort tasks like reading, listening to music, or making a meal with your family.

Emotional: Stress comes with the life of an athlete. To manage it well, limit negative messages from social media while increasing positive social connections. Take your boundaries seriously. If a friend needs help, but your emotional battery is low, take a step back and let them know you'll get back to them later. To unwind, engage in a hobby not tied to external rewards.[43]

Spiritual: No matter your beliefs, taking care of your spiritual side or your soul is essential for peace of mind. Whether this means prioritizing worship for a specific religion or engaging in meditation, spiritual well-being keeps you focused on your purpose. This can even look like journaling and self-reflection.

Social: Isolating yourself is never good. Make sure you balance your sport with a healthy social life by adding it to a routine.[44] Keep a couple of days in your week free for outings and socializing. Stay connected via texting, calls, and social media. Consider joining a club or keeping close ties with other athletes in your field.

Above all, make sure you have a balanced lifestyle.[45] Too much of anything, even the good stuff, can destabilize you.

General tip: Make it a habit to ask yourself, "Is this helping me or harming me?"

To help guide you in answering this question, regularly check in with yourself every week and note the actions you take or habits you engage in. Then, compare it to your higher self: the best version of the champion you imagine yourself to become throughout the journey to your goal. Compare: do your current actions align with the best version?

Another way of looking at this is to focus on the things that bring you immense joy, contentment, satisfaction, and a sense of purpose. Then, try to increase more of those activities. Whether that means surpassing your limit in the gym's weight room or flying across the track, do more to chase that feeling of passion. Don't get stuck in the tediousness of the sport but have more moments of enjoyment.

What do you do about the stuff that's hurting you?

If your actions or habits are not helpful or even detrimental, make a plan to change them.[46]

This is not easy since some habits are hardwired. However, you must *use your goal to motivate your change*. Without motivation, it will be hard to keep up a major renovation in the habits that keep you from meeting your goal.

We are constantly changing anyway. You may as well direct those changes yourself by increasing the actions that are helping you and reducing what is not.

When to Ask for Help

Just because it's your goal doesn't mean you have to go about it alone. Nearly all of the best athletes worldwide had a mentor or coach whom they looked up to or had their family and friends backing them. Being independent in sports may leave you isolated and fumbling for resources. Asking for help can save you some much-needed time.

That said, asking for help is hard.

Maybe pride is holding you back, or the fear of embarrassment or burdening another person. Don't worry—if it's the right person, they will be happy to help. If they aren't, there are plenty of other people.

To ask for help the right way, keep the following tips in mind:[47]

1. Don't be sorry about it. Everyone asks for help sometimes, so there's no need to be overly apologetic.
2. As a common courtesy, try to ask for help face-to-face. Doing so in person ensures you communicate your message and your needs properly.
3. There's no need to offer anything in return since that cheapens your request.

4. When asking for help, try to be as honest as possible. People can't fully help you if they don't know what's going on. Don't beat around the bush; be direct about the problem, why it's important, and how they can help.

5. Finally, show that you have honored the person by updating them on the impact of their help. This is a better way of expressing gratitude than a simple thank you.

Try this: Now it's time to assess what might be breaking you down and what you can do about it. Create a personal growth plan that intertwines all facets of your life: career, self-improvement, education, and social life.[48]

Figure out your what, why, and how.

- What? The specific goals you're aiming for.
- Why? The purpose or reason why the goals are important for you.
- How? The step-by-step plan for carrying out your plan and how to bypass the things that might prevent you from doing so.

So you've figured out what is holding you back. You are actively taking steps to combat it. Now, it's time to focus on the positive aspects of your life: the things that bring you purpose and build you up.

4

KNOW WHAT BUILDS YOU UP

"Learn to be what you are, and learn to resign with a good grace all that you are not."

— HENRI FRÉDÉRIC AMIEL

Getting rid of anything that holds you back is one side of the coin. Afterward, it's time to be all you are to the fullest. That means maximizing what builds you up.

SURESHOT TECHNIQUE #3: KNOW WHAT IS GOOD FOR YOU

Surfer Bethany Hamilton learned to surf at an early age.[49] Being a Hawaii native, the waves were her second home. Things turned south during an unexpected shark attack. Left with only one arm, Bethany was forced to come to terms with her new life.

At this point, she had two options. She could have taken her injury as a sign that she would never surf again. Or, she could have held a long period of pity, feeling sorry for herself before eventually trying to surf again when she gets her morale back.

Which one did she choose?

Bethany immediately jumped back into surfing without wasting time feeling sorry for herself. She saw her injury for what it really was: a challenge, not a limitation. It made her think out of the box to relearn surfing with one arm. Who said you needed both, right?

Developing mental toughness means being willing to learn from challenges. It's about chasing self-growth by using a problem as a stepping stone to success. Of course, this isn't one-size-fits-all. You'll have to find the right coping skills and strategies to be mentally tough.

However, there are some foundational skills that can help build you up, even in your lowest moments:

1. Build self-worth
2. Surround yourself with supportive people
3. Learn to make good choices
4. Practice keystone habits

Implementing these things into your life will create a robust mental defense system. This will help you fight against self-doubt, physical challenges, psychological obstacles, and anything standing in your path of athletic success.

Build Self-Worth

Self-worth is how much value you assign to yourself.[50] Having low self-worth can come from not having a strong inner foundation. Perhaps you need external validation to feel good about yourself. Because of this, your self-esteem might be low and easily shaken by mishaps.

Here are some clues that you suffer from low self-worth:

- Negative self-talk
- Ignoring the positives in your life
- Highlighting the negatives
- Jumping to conclusions
- Black-and-white thinking

A healthy level of self-worth leads to confidence in your skills and capabilities.[51] You can build and maintain positive relationships. Criticism does not bother you as much as it allows you the opportunity to learn. Moreover, good self-worth provides opportunities to grow in your skills. After all, you believe that with practice, you can continually improve.

When you strengthen your self-worth, you'll notice that:

- Old triggers no longer affect you
- You can view situations more logically
- Forgiving yourself for a mistake is easier
- You move on quickly from failure by recognizing the lesson
- You can become your own cheerleader

Strong self-worth is the base level we all need to be at before we can move on to toughening our minds. For a stronger sense of self-worth, there are a few things you can do:

1. Identify and Challenge Negative Beliefs
2. Identify the Positive about Yourself
3. Build Positive Relationships
4. Give Yourself a Break
5. Become More Assertive
6. Improve Your Physical Health
7. Take on Challenges

Let's go through each strategy so you can learn to apply it in your life.

Identify and Challenge Negative Beliefs

The negative beliefs you have were not decided by you. You've come to have certain beliefs about yourself from the messages you absorbed as a child from your parents, teachers, friends, society, media, and others. These beliefs may or may not be true. All we know is that negative beliefs are often damaging and can keep you stuck with low self-esteem.

Research tells us that negative beliefs actually limit our opportunities. If you don't believe in yourself, chances are that you will not take a chance. However, if you believe you can do something —whether the belief is objectively true or not—you are likely to take more risks. You are then more likely to end up with wonderful opportunities.

In the sports world, athletes have no choice but to believe in themselves. Low self-esteem will only bog you down with extra unnecessary baggage. Physically, you might take one step forward, but your negative beliefs might hold you back from four extra steps. You don't want to miss out on progress, especially not if you're the obstacle standing in your way.

What are your negative beliefs about yourself? To take control of your self-esteem, you have to think about why you currently feel the way you do. What conscious or subconscious beliefs do you have about your abilities?

Here are some common negative beliefs that athletes may suffer from. You might resonate with some of these:

1. I'm not as good as others in my sport.
2. I don't feel like a real basketball/soccer/football player, boxer, gymnast, swimmer, etc.
3. I might let my team and/or coach down.
4. What if I just don't have the talent, no matter how hard I try?
5. I'm afraid of embarrassing myself in front of everyone.

If any of those rang a bell, try taking out a trusty journal and jotting them down. Journaling is often the go-to method of getting deep and dark with ourselves. When you free-write about a personal topic, your hand magically comes up with a realization you never considered before. Now, you'll do the same to understand and *challenge* your negative beliefs.

To recap, here's the step-by-step guide:

1. Identify your negative beliefs and make a list.
2. Pick your top five negative beliefs.
3. On separate pages, write each of the five beliefs at the top.
4. For each belief, write a sentence answering the following: a) Why do you think you believe it? b) What evidence do you have for it in your daily life? c) Is there any evidence against the belief in your daily

life? d) Is it useful for you to continue believing in this negative belief? e)What would your life look like if you believed the opposite?

5. On another paper, or better yet, a post-it note, flip those negative beliefs to their positive alternatives. (i.e., "It takes me such a long time to master a new technique; I'm falling behind." → "No matter how long it takes, I commit to mastering every technique I learn. I'm exactly where I'm supposed to be in my journey.")

Identify the Positive About Yourself

One of the best ways to strengthen self-worth is to remember what's amazing about you. Then, aim to use those positives to their fullest advantage.

Go back to your journal and write a list of all your positives. Maybe you're a natural-born leader or ambitious. Whatever it may be, jot down as many as you can think of. Then, pick your top five, whether it's your favorite quality about yourself or your strongest one. Now, brainstorm at least three ways you can maximize each positive trait. How can you involve it more in your life and athletic career? In your relationships? How can you build on it? Doubling down on what's great about you gives you a stronger sense of self. Knowing what you bring to the table can help you build confidence.

Build Positive Relationships

Relationships (positive relationships) will always build you up, especially when it comes to self-esteem. You will know you have an extraordinary relationship with someone if you leave every interaction feeling secure and good about yourself.

Part of this is putting in your effort to build a more positive relationship. Having self-worth is not just about validation or what others can give you. You'll find a greater sense of self-satisfaction if you also invest in a worthy friendship.

To build more positive relationships:

- Give your time to the right people. Reach out to them first and keep in touch.
- Be more open and expressive with people you feel comfortable with.
- Offer to do kind services without conditions.
- Aim to understand before focusing on being understood.
- Respect others' boundaries.

Athletes are not lone wolves. Whether it's teammates, club members, or a personal social circle, relationships give athletes an extra reason to do their best.

Give Yourself a Break

Mentally tough people are not mean or self-deprecating. You must be compassionate to build your self-worth. Treat yourself as you would treat a friend or family. Being too hard on another will never allow them to feel good about themselves. The same goes for you.

That said, remember to give yourself a break. We are all human. Making a mistake is no reason to get down on yourself, whether in life or sports. As an athlete, you understand the importance of rest and recovery.

Become More Assertive

How you respect yourself and your time is an indicator of your self-worth. Being assertive shows that you respect yourself and others. This looks like saying no to requests you can take on. If you feel like you have to say yes, it means your self-worth is on the lower end. No one *has to* say yes to *everything*. Uphold your boundaries by standing your ground when it comes to your decisions.

Improve Your Physical Health

Overall physical health does contribute to good self-worth, believe it or not. The respect you give to your body often mirrors how you value yourself. Unfortunately, neglecting your diet, sleep, or other health needs is not an indicator of self-respect. It usually means you are prioritizing other things in your life.

Even putting your sport first before your health is a problem. Not only are you disrespecting your body, but you are also disrespecting your sport by failing to be in good physical shape to take it on. Every success expert will tell you that taking care of yourself comes first, and success will follow. Make sure to improve your physical health so you feel good enough naturally to take on the day.

Take on Challenges

Challenging yourself on your own terms helps break you out of your comfort zone. When you overcome those challenges, you feel more competent and confident in your ability. If you struggle with a challenge several times, it gives you information about what you can do better next time.

Overall, taking on challenges promises an experience that will build character, self-worth, and self-assurance. If you ever face a challenge, be it a difficult game or a conflict between teammates, try to see it in a better light. After the challenge passes, you will most likely be glad it occurred. It makes you stronger and better at what you do. If you know this, then you may as well feel grateful for the challenge from the beginning. This perspective shift can change how you approach it.

Surround Yourself With Supportive People

A common saying is that you are the average of the several people you spend your time with. While that's debatable, it brings up a good point. The people who surround us can make or break us. As much as we like to think we have full control over our feelings and behaviors, our friends can be really influential. What we do have control over is what type of influence we want: positive or negative. A bad friend can leave you feeling even worse about your situation or guilty about spending time on your athletic goals. A good friend is supportive, no matter what, as long as you are doing what's right for you.

How can you tell if a person is worth spending time with?[52]

There are a few signs to look out for:

1. **Honesty**: Good friends are open and communicative. They don't beat around the bush. If they have an issue with the relationship, they aren't passive-aggressive or leave you feeling guilty about something you're not sure you did.
2. **Kindness:** A genuinely kind person will offer to pay for your meal without asking for the money back later. They are kind both in public and behind closed doors.
3. **Thoughtfulness:** For someone to be supportive, they must be interested in understanding and considering others' feelings. A good friend will be thoughtful and consider how their words and actions may affect you. They will put effort into empathizing with you and seeing your perspective.

4. **Respect boundaries:** Boundaries are helpful because they are like a "good friend screener." If you assert your boundaries to someone and they do not respect you, you immediately know not to waste your time. A worthwhile friend will always listen and respect your boundaries.[53]

5. **Brings you comfort:** You should not be feeling nervous or self-conscious while meeting up with a good friend. Supportive friends will be easy to be around. Whether they are naturally comforting or take consideration of your needs, such people are the ones you should stick around.[54]

Learn to Make Good Choices

How do you know if you are making good choices? It can be a difficult thing to measure. However, there are tools you can use to improve your decision-making process.[55]

1. Imagine yourself a year in the future. This visualization practice helps you figure out what choices you need to make to get to your ideal place.

2. Write down your goals. To ensure you stick to your value-based purpose, keep track of your goals. Daily, weekly, monthly, and yearly goals remind you of what's important. When you go back to them, you can clarify a difficult decision.

3. Compare the choices you have. Create a pros and cons list for each potential choice. If it's not helping,

think outside the box. There may be other choices you have yet to consider.

4. Is there something you don't know? Seek information. Maybe you're missing a critical piece of the puzzle that can make the decision simpler.

5. Become objective. Step away and look at the big picture. Sometimes, it's easier for others to see the right choice for you, even when you can't see it. That's because you're too close, too wrapped up in your head. Distance yourself and see the big picture. In other words, forget about yourself for a second. If you didn't care about your pride, success, money, or societal expectations, what would be the right choice in the long run?

6. Consider mistakes you've made and find the lesson. We've all made choices we regretted in the past. Don't let them go to waste. Remember what you learned from those "bad choices," as that information can help you cancel out the choices you definitely wouldn't want.

7. Ask supportive, trusted people for advice and feedback. The people who know you well might give you a fresh perspective on what might be right for you.

8. Look at the long-term and short-term implications. Make sure you're not sacrificing long-term success for short-term instant gratification. Always think of choices as

investments. Will your final decision get you the best return on investment?

At the end of the day, remember this: indecision is unnecessary. Indecision comes from doubt or fear of making the wrong choice. Yet there is no wrong choice. The fact of the matter is that whatever you choose will be right for you. Moreover, your life will fall in line to align with your choice.

If you make a "bad" choice, meaning a choice you regret, use it as a lesson for the next. Do not, under any circumstance, ruminate about it. Even "bad" choices were the right ones for you because they helped you learn something.

Practice Keystone Habits

Keystone habits are the important habits in anyone's life that are a part of your routine.[56] If any of these habits are missing or not done well, it can create a domino effect across your other habits and overall well-being. For instance, a diet full of junk, sugary drinks, or skipped meals will affect your energy, sleep hygiene, and stress levels. If you do not do certain keystone habits, like self-care or planning, it leaves you even more stressed and likely to get overwhelmed.

Keystone habits include:

- Healthy diet
- Healthy sleep routine
- Exercise

- Planning
- Self-care
- Meditation

Research has shown that building positive habits is better than just focusing on self-control. Don't rely on sheer willpower. That will tire you out and lead to inconsistent efforts. Instead, focus on improving these foundational habits.

How to Make Habits That Stick

Start by checking in with yourself. What does your current routine look like? Identify the habits you do on a daily basis without even realizing it. Consider if they are helping you or making your life worse.

For example, if the first thing you do after coming from afterschool training is to take a nap, think about how it is affecting your life. Maybe it messes up your sleep schedule, prevents you from doing homework on time, and leaves you tired in the morning. Instead, after training, you can have a healthy high-protein snack and some fruit before getting your homework out of the way. Some simple shifts and rearranging can change the rest of your lifestyle.

Now, you might have a lot of habits to work on. There is a systematic way to stick to your habit changes.[57] First, start by replacing bad habits. Pick one habit at a time and make small, doable adjustments. Second, decide to follow this new habit and commit to your decision. Save yourself some grief by identifying potential triggers and obstacles to carrying out this habit. Habits are dictated by environmental or emotional triggers. For instance, you might have a habit of reaching for sugary snacks when sad. Consider what triggers your bad habits and create a plan to avoid said triggers or cope with them better. Always plan to succeed but prepare to fail.

When successful, reward yourself, potentially right after you complete the daily habit. Rewards encourage the habit and make it something to look forward to.

Get support from your family and friends for the obstacles out of your control or the days when your will is not at full power.

Finally, celebrate small wins after a couple of weeks or a month of keeping the new habit up.

Try this: Pick *one* keystone habit and create a plan. How will you add it to your life?[58]

1. Choose a trigger that signals this habit.
2. Consider a reward to give yourself to reinforce this habit.
3. Create a support system. Get rid of what might keep you from following this habit and inform friends and family so they may support you.

4. Track your habit daily on your phone or in a journal to see your progress.

5. At the end of the first two weeks, reflect. How has this habit contributed to your growth? Did it help build you up?

Practicing habit-building will show you how much power you *can* have over yourself. The truth is that you can master what goes on in your mind. Find out how in the next chapter.

5

INSIDE YOUR MIND

"From the neck up is where you win or lose the battle. It's the art of war. You have to lock yourself in and strategize your mindset. That's why boxers go to training camps: to shut down the noise and really zone in."

— ANTHONY JOSHUA

SURESHOT TECHNIQUE #4: MASTER YOUR MIND AND YOUR MINDSET

Muhammad Ali was an exceptional boxer.[59] But he didn't get there without having to take risks along the way. He had to make friends with risk in a time of racial segregation. When it feels like the world is against you, it can be hard to rise up and pave your own path. But Muhammad Ali did just that.

It started when his bike got stolen as a young teenager. Most people would lament the problem, maybe save some money and get a new bike. Perhaps a privileged few would report it to the police. However, remember that as an African-American, Muhammad Ali did not have those resources available to him at the time. He was on his own.

From there on, he was inspired to learn to fight so that he could take care of himself in case anyone threatened him or his possessions again. Imagine: he couldn't rely on the system, and he couldn't rely on anyone else. Anyone in this situation would understandably succumb to the environment. Yet, Ali aimed to do one thing that would always be in his control: fight back.

Ali's story is an example of how perspective can change *everything*.

The Power of Perspective

Perspective makes an enormous difference in how a situation will affect your feelings, reactions, and behaviors.[60] For example, your coach approaches you to discuss your recent performance. He says it relatively respectfully, starting with positive, then mentioning some things you could work on. Depending on your perspective, you may leave the conversation feeling good or low. Perhaps you only focus on the positive, ignore the negative, and continue making the same mistake. Alternatively, you may focus on the negative and feel like you're constantly disappointing people. There are many more potential reactions you may have to this situation; the point is that while the situation is the same in all scenarios, the only difference is how you perceive it.

Perspective usually is based on two things: your reasoning for why something happened and what it means to you.

When faced with negative criticism, some might reason it's because they suck as an athlete or because their coach is out to get them. Both of these reasons could drive someone to focus only on the negative. Additionally, such a situation might be more meaningful to some than others. The more meaningful it is, the more powerful the emotions that drive someone's perspective—good or bad.

Moreover, how you rationalize a situation and its meaningfulness depends on your experience. People who are used to feedback might not ascribe that much importance to their coach's feedback. They might view it positively. However, those with a history of perfectionism and low self-esteem might feel like it's the end of the world.

The point is that there are infinite possibilities for a person's perspective.

The great news is that you don't have to be a victim. Perspective is changeable with conscious decisions and actions, and you can always take back the driver's seat.

To do that, it's necessary to master your thoughts.

How to Master Your Thoughts

A false notion many people have is that thoughts are uncontrollable. In reality, not all of your thoughts can be trusted. Many of them are based on old patterns or out-of-date beliefs. Nearly all are not based on facts. Such thoughts can muddle our minds, creating misinterpretations or inaccurate conclusions.

As athletes, you must not only improve the skills your sport demands but also your mind. A positive mentality is what will allow you to keep leveling up. The right mentality starts with managing your thoughts.

To do that, try the following:

- Come to terms with the fact that your thoughts are not always true. They can be changed if you choose —by changing your perspective.

- Focus on observing yourself rather than judging. Be nonjudgmentally curious about how you think and feel. For instance, rather than judging: "I feel frustrated about my low performance today. I'm losing my skill as an athlete." Observe: "I am feeling frustrated because of my low performance. I don't have to think or act on that feeling. I can sit with it until it passes."

With time, you can become more objective. Sometimes it's easier to see a situation as not as bad from an outside point of view looking in. Or you may see solutions you didn't see before. The key is to distance yourself from your thoughts. This builds awareness of yourself, which proves to you that you choose to accept or not accept your thoughts, after all.

Develop Mindfulness

The fast-paced modern world makes it hard to simply be aware of the moment and deliberately pay attention. Our minds are scattered and pulled apart by many things in our lives that fight for our attention. Unfortunately, this means we miss out on the benefits of mindfulness.[61] With it, we can achieve incredible control over our minds.

Luckily, mindfulness is a skill you get better at every time you practice it. And the better you are, the more mastery you will have over your thoughts, feelings, and actions.

Here are some excellent mindfulness exercises:[62]

1. Practice focusing on a *single* thing at any given time.
2. Every day, aim to notice one thing for a few minutes *nonjudgmentally*.
3. Get in touch with your senses.
4. Practice *describing* your state without criticizing it. Often, our problems come from not accepting how we're feeling. Maybe we are unmotivated to put real effort into training, and we feel guilty or angry at ourselves for feeling that way. Cut through the noise by simply explaining how you feel without making it negative or positive. Describe it mentally or write it out, and don't mention how you "should" feel. Discuss the physical and mental sensations of the emotion. This is an exploration, a way of being mindful of your experience with *acceptance*, which can be uncomfortable at first.

Battle Your Negative Inner Critic

Self-talk is exactly as it sounds. It's the voice inside your head that you use when talking to yourself. In psychology, self-talk is so important because of its tremendous impact. Negative self-talk can be the same as always having a verbally abusive friend or parent over your shoulder.[59] It can lead to chronic stress, depression, low self-esteem, and stunted growth in your athletic goals.

If your inner critic is hard to pinpoint, keep an eye out for any sign of negativity from that voice. Things like, "I can't do this," or "If it's not perfect, I shouldn't bother," are some common signs.[63]

Over time, you will realize that there are two of you in your head—that critic and the real you. The more you notice the critic, the stronger the 'real you' becomes. This is because you are feeling that separation from the negative self-talk more and more.

It helps to name this inner character. Make it a ridiculous caricature that you can easily dismiss.

One way to battle your inner critic is to stay present.[64] Keep your mind in the here and now as much as possible. The "present" state is often what many athletes call the flow state, when you are in the midst of performing, and your body and mind are in sync with the movements, the game, or the sport. Your brain is not on autopilot—it is completely centered on the moment right in front of you. It's an exhilarating sort of calm where the magic happens.

Along with being in the present, it's vital to replace the critic. Replace that voice with an encouraging friend or a neutral, objective logistician. The 'friend' voice can be modeled after a real person in your life. Consider what they may say in place of your critic. As for the neutral logistician, simply shift your negative language to more neutral language.

For example:

- "This is so difficult." → "I would rather not . . ."
- "I'm going to fail." → "I'm not sure how I'll do . . ."
- "I have no chance at winning." → "Realistically, there is a chance I might win or lose."

This technique lessens the power of negativity and makes the situation bearable and realistic. It's a stepping stone to positivity. Sometimes it feels fake to jump from pessimism to optimism—like we're lying to ourselves. With neutrality, we acknowledge our opinion or emotion while still knowing that we can undergo the situation anyway.

Examine Your Thoughts

Are your thoughts helping you or limiting you? A mentally strong person knows how to guide their thoughts down the right path. The right path leads to their ultimate goal or aspiration. They know that if they want to stick to their commitment, their thoughts need to be helping them. If any thought is not helpful to the cause, it needs to get kicked out.

How do you know whether a thought is true or not?

Look for the facts that support the thought and the facts that are against it.[65]

Consider an alternate universe in which you *didn't think* this thought. What would you do? How would you feel?

In summary:

1. Is this thought a fact?
2. If yes, what evidence can back up the thought?
3. Can you find any evidence to oppose the thought?
4. What if you didn't think this thought? What would you think otherwise?
5. How would you feel, and what would you do if you did not think this thought?

Reframe Your Thoughts

Changing your thoughts overnight isn't realistic. However, you can at least get in the habit of asking yourself a crucial question: how could you think about this situation differently?

Reframing thoughts is about considering alternative ways of looking at things.[66] It's actually the main idea of Cognitive-Behavioral Therapy.[67] If you now know that maybe not all of your thoughts are true, you're going to have to think outside the box.

Mindfulness is the first start. It helps you stay aware of thoughts that are not helpful. When you get used to catching them, you can begin to replace them with helpful ones. With enough repetitive action, your brain will become accustomed to thinking more helpful thoughts than unhelpful thoughts, and it will become a habit.

Another thing to remember is that sometimes the truth doesn't matter. Rather than wonder if a thought has enough evidence, consider how useful it is to you. If it's only causing anxiety and distress, it's not as useful. That means it's time to consider more useful ways of reframing the thought.[68]

For instance, try observing your thoughts as follows:[69]

You get the thought, "My coach just said my time for this run is less than usual. I'm totally going to come in last at the next track meet."

Is this thought helpful? You are jumping to some severe conclusions. It's making you even more stressed over the meet, which could impact your focus, health, and performance. How could you reframe it to make the thought more helpful?

Try: "Whatever the outcome of the next track meet is, I'm eager to return to my original record and even surpass my normal. In fact, I'm glad for this challenge because I've been stagnant for a while. This is an opportunity to reach for a better personal goal."

Master Your Focus

Focus is a keystone skill in sports. If the noise of daily life is too loud, it can become a barrier in your athletic career. What you focus on is what you pour energy and effort into. That means you must hone this skill, which is not that complex. Attention span is not a talent that some have, and others don't. The more you practice it, the better you get.

To master your focus, do the following steps:

- Meditation
- Conscious Focus Exercises
- Stop Multitasking

Meditation

How does meditation improve focus? The whole point of meditation is to reduce mind-wandering.[70] You sit still and try to pay attention to your breath. Every time you find your mind getting away from you, you return your focus back to the breath as soon as you become aware.

In this way, meditation exercises two muscles: self-awareness (your ability to notice what you are doing at any moment) and attention skills. The first time you meditate, your mind might wander every fifteen seconds. The tenth time you meditate, your mind might wander every minute, which means you have now increased your attention span.

Conscious Focus Exercises

Focus exercises are challenging tasks that improve concentration, recall, and overall mental clarity.[71] The more you exercise, the longer you can devote mental energy to a task.

The following are some helpful focus exercises you can start now:

1. Read a book.
2. Try active listening.
3. Concentrate on doing one physical activity during a period of time without stopping.
4. Do crossword puzzles.
5. Try challenging counting games. Count backward from a high number like 100 or 500. Try counting every other number or skipping every three numbers. Practice recalling the multiplication table.

Stop Multitasking

Multitasking is a productivity killer. Even doing two easy tasks simultaneously does not offer any time-saving benefits. This is because when you are multitasking, your brain has to work hard to switch between tasks. That task-switching process takes much longer and uses more energy than you think. That means the quality of each task might not be as good if you'd done it alone. Moreover, you'll feel more tired on a daily basis, which is not what we want if our goal is to tackle every day successfully.[72]

If there's one thing you should do to improve your focus, it's to cut out multitasking. Here's what you can do:

- Turn off your phone or notifications while working so you don't get interrupted.
- Keep your workspace empty except for what you need at that given moment.
- Instead of saying "yes" to a request when you're unsure or busy, say that you'll think about it. This ensures you have control over your time.
- Divide activities by environment or location. Your desk is now only for homework, not for playing games. Your bed is only for sleeping. The couch in your living room can be dedicated to lounging and taking a fun break.
- Start planning your day. This way, you don't get to the point where you feel you need to multitask to get everything done.

Do What's in Front of You

The path to reaching your goal is long. Being spread too thin at any given moment doesn't help you get there faster. The best way to get there is to do one thing at a time. Being present in the moment and focusing on what is in front of you will grow your willpower.

Tip #1: Change how you think about what's in front of you. Rather than seeing it as a huge feat, break it down. Take it one step at a time, one task at a time. Don't think about the hill or mountain; laser-focus on every single step. To practice that focus, try what productivity experts call *chunking.*

Time chunking is breaking your schedule or a set period of time into doable chunks in which you *only* carry out what you need to do.[73]

For instance, do you want a more productive gym session? Cut your gym time into chunks of 10 or 15 minutes (depending on your workout), and in each chunk, fill it up with the hardest work you possibly can. If you're doing cardio, don't stop until the chunk time is up. If you're working out with weights, concentrate on only that exercise during the set time. If you're practicing basketball hoops, don't stop shooting until the time is up. This stretches your mind to not even think about breaks until the chunk time is over.

Want to cut down time on your schoolwork? Organize your homework and study sessions into chunks of 25 minutes with 5-minute breaks in between. Not only does this force you to face the work you need to do with undivided attention, but it's also better for your energy. Research shows that regular, short breaks can rejuvenate the mind's energy so you can keep going for longer.

Remember: for chunking to work, you cannot do anything else but the chosen task. Gradually, you chip away at the huge task by doing bite-sized tasks.

Tip #2: Always finish what you start. If there's one principle you should add to your life, it's this one. Training yourself not to stop until the job is done increases willpower.[74]

Most of us get used to leaving things off if it gets boring or too difficult. Unfortunately, that teaches you to stop when things get hard, the opposite of resilience. It's vital to rewire those habits.

Retrain your brain to go past your limits by deciding to always complete the projects you begin. Making this decision means you will think more critically about the tasks you take on. You will be able to choose the high-priority tasks that are worth completing. Plus, having a track record of completed tasks gives you a greater sense of purpose and pride.

Tip #3: Look forward to exciting things.[75] You don't need to wait for exceptional things to happen in life. We always have the choice to change our perspective about each day.

For example, we can decide to wake up eagerly for the day to unfold. Each person can think of their own reasons why. When you do some thinking, you'll find there's a lot more to look forward to than you realize. Consciously waking up every morning with those things in mind fills you with purpose, awareness, and motivation. More importantly, you stop living in automatic mode: waking up in a fog, plodding through the day, just trying to get it over with. Instead, school becomes full of excitement, sports training becomes meaningful and inspiring, and you savor the small things you enjoy even more.

Challenge yourself every day for a week or more to come up with three things you're excited about every morning. See how it changes the quality of life without you having to make a major shift.

Tip #4: Connect your daily tasks to a greater purpose.[76] Remember the direction you chose regarding your sports goal? I'm willing to bet your direction is based on a bigger purpose, even if you're not sure what it is. You want to build mental toughness for a reason—to live meaningfully. One way to do that is to make every tedious task meaningful.

Often our physical exercises are a symbol. They represent something greater than becoming faster or stronger. When you train as an athlete, you are preparing your body and mind for the harsh side of life. It's a tangible way to measure how much you can take.

It doesn't stop there. In life, anything can be a training. Think of ancient folk stories where the main character is forced to do menial tasks before moving to the next level. The lesson is that if you don't see that value in what you must do—dishes, maths, chores, errands—you're letting these things go to waste. You get the value that is assigned. If you view doing dishes as a training for becoming mentally stronger or as a stepping stone to your greater goal, you'll never do them the same again.

Try this: Now, take account of your current mindset. Are you calm, stressed, overwhelmed, content, or frustrated?

Positive or negative, take a minute to observe your thoughts and feelings. Rate your negative emotion (if any) from 1–10. Try one of the tips mentioned in this chapter for a few minutes. Go ahead.

When you are done, check again and rate your negative emotion.

Practice doing this exercise during high stress moments in your athletic journey. Always measure before and after to see that it really works.

Controlling your emotions can feel like a huge feat. Yet it can be done. The even better news? If you cannot handle your emotions, you can definitely channel them into additional energy to perform better.

6

EMOTIONAL ENERGY

"I don't want to be at the mercy of my emotions. I want to use them, to enjoy them, and to dominate them."

— OSCAR WILDE

E motions aren't all bad. Being mentally strong is not about shutting down your emotions; it's about reining them and using them for a better purpose. Moreover, being good at a sport isn't just about skill, talent, or hard work. Countless athletes have deep, powerful inner emotions driving them.

SURESHOT TECHNIQUE #5: MASTER YOUR EMOTIONS AND USE THEIR ENERGY TO DRIVE YOU FORWARD

Olympics champion Michael Phelps is one of the most well-known swimmers worldwide—and for a good reason. He broke many world records, all in a single Olympics game.[77] But did you know that Michael suffered from ADHD for most of his childhood and young adult life?

ADHD can make it difficult for anyone to function in their day-to-day routine. It's a brain disorder that can mess with a person's attention span and ability to stay on task. It may involve restless, unending energy and impulsive behavior. All of these could have prevented Michael from performing his best. For instance, ADHD symptoms can get in the way of following a set schedule, managing one's time, staying focused, finishing a task, etc.

How did Michael push through his swimming career despite ADHD? Simple. He worked *with* it rather than *against* it.

As a swimmer, Michael knew that swimming against the tide never works—a swimmer must harmonize with the water. He looked past the dark side of ADHD and focused on what he could work with. Many people forget that another key symptom of ADHD is hyperfocus regarding specific tasks. If someone with ADHD has a special interest or hobby, they can access unlimited attention and focus.

Being passionate about swimming, Michael poured all of his restless energy into training. His love for the sport made him hyperfocus effortlessly, leading him to surpass the average in his field.

Anyone can do this, ADHD or not. With the power of strong emotion, you, too, can fuel yourself with more energy than you thought possible.

A Crash Course on Emotions

Emotions and feelings are not the same thing.[78] Feelings are what we talk about when we describe our subjective experience of a situation. They are often based on conscious thought. For example, "I feel sad" or "I'm so happy." Emotions are subconscious physiological states that impact the body's biology, and we may or may not be aware of them.

We can pinpoint them by assessing the bodily sensations. For instance, you may feel the emotion of anger through a high body temperature, fast heart rate, and rapid breathing.

The foundational emotions include fear, disgust, anger, contempt, surprise, sadness, and joy.

Additionally, there are more specific secondary emotions. For instance, anger can arise as rage, irritation, or exasperation. Sadness can range from mild disappointment to shame. Joy's secondary emotions include contentment, pride, and relief.

Emotions act like a communication channel between our bodies and minds.[79] They are primarily not in control because they are based on signals the body receives from the environment that help us follow our survival instincts.

Why do we take emotions seriously if they aren't in our control? While thoughts can drive our feelings, unconscious emotions also influence our thoughts, perspectives, and behaviors.[80] Our conscious minds try to translate the physiological messages of emotions. However, our translation might not be so accurate.

Based on how we read our emotions, we take specific actions. In other words, although unconscious emotions are not in our control, we can manage how we perceive and act on them.

Emotions as Tools for Life Changes

Ignoring emotions doesn't work. If we aren't aware of how our emotions affect us, we won't be able to use them to our advantage. Instead, emotions will direct how our life unfolds, whether we accept it or not.[81] The key is to be in harmony with emotions. Understanding your emotional state and then responding mindfully is a superpower.

Understand that most of the time, you are picking up on the secondary emotion, not the basic emotion.

How to Master Emotions

To improve performance, athletes must be masters of their emotions—not emotionless, but rulers of their emotional state. During a time of incredible racial violence in America's history emerged the first black heavyweight boxing champion—Jack Johnson.

Johnson was a cutting example of emotional mastery. Because of his color, he was booed and laughed at every time he stepped into the ring. Crowds would always root for his white opponent. It wasn't that this didn't bother him, but during this time, there wasn't much Johnson could do. Complain? Yell? Tell them to stop? Quit? It was a difficult period. Johnson had to do what he could with what he had.

What did he do? He wiped all emotions from his face and operated like a cool boxing robot. If he let the crowd's boos get to him, he lost. Instead, he won what he could—the match.

Use the following techniques to master your emotions:

Identify Emotions

Ever noticed that most athletes are very in touch with their emotions? On the outside, they look stoic and fearless, but they know exactly what their emotion is and channel it in other ways. You can learn to do that, too, with the following practices:[81]

- Name your feelings: Awareness starts by noticing and naming what you feel. Whether you feel anxious before a performance, disappointed after a failure, or overwhelmed, simply name it.

- Expand your emotional vocabulary to better express yourself: Sometimes we can't really pinpoint what we're feeling. That leaves us feeling even more frustrated. To address this, learn more terminologies to describe a varied emotional experience. Instead of just having one word for feeling angry, you could describe it as slightly irked or absolutely furious.

- Track emotions in your journal: Keep track of how you feel daily in a journal or on your phone's notes app. Expressing your emotions through writing is cathartic. Moreover, it helps you know what your usual emotions are and why they occur if you track them on a daily basis.

Don't Act on Emotions Immediately

It takes a few moments for an emotion to sink in. So it's best to postpone acting on them immediately, as immediate actions can lead to rash decisions you might regret. Athletes know that staying calm is vital during high-stakes moments like a competition, show, or sporting event.

There are several tricks to calm down both emotionally and physiologically.[81] The first one is self-explanatory—*breathe.* When you are highly emotional, it triggers your sympathetic nervous system—that's the fight-or-flight response. In other words, you'll feel your heart pounding, sweating, and breathing too fast. If you can't immediately calm down with soothing thoughts, target it physically. Deep breathing is the best way to go because breathing controls other symptoms.

Respond, Don't React

What's the difference between responding and reacting? A reaction is an instantaneous act triggered by a situation. A response is something you choose to provide after deliberate thought. The two are best differentiated by the time and space between a trigger and the action to address the trigger. Responding has a longer duration between an emotional trigger and an actual action. During that time, you are distancing yourself from subjective emotion to a more objective, rational mindset.[82]

Why should you respond instead of reacting? Well, it's simple: ideally, we want to make decisions with a clear mind. When emotions color our thoughts, our mind is anything but clear. It's tainted and swirling with irrationality. Lacking mental clarity leads to reacting to the dominant emotion you experience.

Here's a simple example. Your team loses a soccer game. The loss is the trigger that fills you with frustration and hot-headed anger. You're filled with the urge to blow up at the other team in that high-intensity moment. If you were to react, you'd go over there right now and throw a tantrum. To respond, however, you would first stop, notice your emotional state, and gain conscious control over your thoughts. That's when you're able to choose the right course of action with a more grounded mind—a mind that recognizes the true consequences and rewards of actions.

The best way to switch from reacting to responding? *Pause.*

Train yourself to stop what you're doing when you experience strong emotions. That simple pause gives you greater awareness of your internal state. Then, you can choose to do whatever you want, whether it's your initial reaction or a new action. Miraculously, you'll find that just a few moments of mindfulness can make a difference in your behavior and life.

The process of getting used to this technique won't be perfect. However, making mistakes is good because the next time you're unable to stop yourself from reacting, you can take notes on the situation. You can learn what emotion led you to the reaction and remember to avoid the same error next time.

Understand the Underlying Need

All emotions are messages. Since the creation of humankind, emotions have served us by offering survival instincts. Our basest emotions allow us to zero in on danger, threats, and avoidance of harm. Other than that, emotions also point to something much deeper about ourselves.

Emotions are triggered by the external environment. Yet how they affect you depends on the underlying needs you lack. These needs are highly individual and depend on a person's upbringing and/or genetics. Often, the things that left an impact on you as a child tend to repeat in your teens and young adulthood. So you might undergo a pattern of similar emotional experiences.

In other words, every emotion has a purpose, especially the ones that come up the most. How they impact you relates to your usual perception of life, your coping mechanism, and your level of resilience. You can also improve your resilience by understanding your emotions. You must be in touch with your emotions to master them, after all.[83]

Since all emotion is a message, you must follow the call deep into your subconscious to see where they stem from. What are they telling you about yourself?

Understand your emotions better by:

- Writing about them: Writing about emotions is more freeing and safer than telling others. You can process how you feel nonjudgmentally. Moreover, writing them down stops rumination in its tracks because you release the emotions driving the thought patterns in your journal.
- Body scan: Bring awareness to your body for sensations you can link to emotion. How does your gut feel? Is your chest tight? Does your blood feel like

it's boiling? Over time, you'll be able to tell what you're feeling right away.

- Observing others: When you observe other people around you or in movies, you can gain more emotional knowledge by how they respond to emotions. The more you get used to how a person's actions relate to their inner world, your empathy for them and yourself grows.

How to Channel Emotions

Being able to channel emotions isn't a myth or a magical superpower that only happens in movies. All emotion is energy, whether it is a positive or negative emotion. When elated, you feel revved up and ready to jump around. When angry, you feel like you could run through a bunch of stone walls and tear them down. The question is, what are you doing with that energy?

If you don't use it properly, that energy can work against us, especially when it comes to negative emotions. We often think that negative emotions are draining. However, how we deal with those emotions is the real problem. It's tempting to push negative emotional states down, but doing so can lead to pent-up energy, which can drain ourselves and everyone around us in the long run. It can lead to irritability, making it difficult for others to be around you, and it can eventually lead to an angry outburst.

What if you could freeze that energy and transform it into something positive? What if you could use it on the court or take it out on the baseball when you swing your bat? Well, you surely can. The trick is to be aware of that energy bubbling up during high emotions.

When you are aware, don't repress it—but save it. Hold the energy at the back of your mind until you get the opportunity to let it out. An opportunity like this might involve any action flourishing with vigorous, emotional energy. Anything creative or athletic benefits from pure emotional energy. Wait until your training session and direct that emotion into your regime. When you make every emotion a part of your purpose, you'll be more motivated to let go of the urge to react instantly.

How to Process and Let Go of Negative Emotions

You don't have to channel all the negative energy that comes your way. Sometimes, letting go of the tension that sticks to your muscles from such emotions is healthy. Specifically, the emotions you've long repressed or pushed back can become a burden on your shoulders. Some might even call it trapped emotion.

Trapped emotion is one way to put it. In reality, any trauma (major or minor) can become cemented in the brain by connecting memory, sensation, and emotion. The stronger the emotion, the more ingrained the memory becomes. When environmental factors trigger those memories, it's like pressing a button that lights up the areas in the brain associated with the trauma. You may even feel it in a specific part of your body.

To release these trapped emotions, you need to process them.[87] Failing to process them is the real reason why they became stuck and built up in the first place.

Try this: Check out these three emotional processing tools and add them to your daily routine:[88]

Tool #1: Quick Stress-Relief With Sensory Information

In the middle of a stressful moment, use this tool to calm you down instantly. Take a deep breath. Then, tune into all of your senses: sight, smell, hearing, touch, and taste. Focusing on the sensory information around you switches your mind from freak-out mode to being more grounded. Thus, it gives you a chance to focus and problem-solve more accurately.

Tool #2: Ride the Wild Horse Meditation

The *Ride the Wild Horse* meditation helps you deal with overwhelming emotions. It's the antidote for people who are chronic avoiders. This meditation is for you if your main coping mechanisms include distraction, ignoring major emotions, or minimizing your problems with jokes. It aims to help you feel intense emotion in a mindful, controlled manner.

Step 1: Start by steadying your breathing.

Step 2: Progressively relax your muscles, starting from the top of your body to the bottom.

Step 3: Now, focus on your emotion and really delve into it. You might get stressed, but if you feel yourself becoming overwhelmed, it's your opportunity to use one of the calming tools you learned.

This meditation offers a safe environment to practice switching to mindfulness during high-emotion moments.

Tool #3: Improve Your Emotional Intelligence

The counterpart to IQ, Emotional Intelligence (EQ), is one's ability to understand and utilize emotions both for personal emotional needs and the needs of others.[89] Emotional intelligence is necessary for effective interpersonal communication. To improve your EQ, you need to focus on four principles:

1. Self-awareness
2. Social awareness
3. Self-management
4. Relationship management

Alongside emotions, you must also ground yourself in the roots of how you are the source of your motivation and strength. Taking care of your spiritual side is just as important for any athlete.

7

THE SOUL OF A SPORTSPERSON

"Never underestimate the power of dreams and the influence of the human spirit. We are all the same in this notion: The potential for greatness lives within each of us."

— WILMA RUDOLPH

As an athlete, your soul is your anchor. Your sport and how you perform are just an extension of your soul. Wherever you go, your soul will be the identifying component of what you do. So if you want to be a truly driven sportsperson, you need to do so for a much greater goal than just worldly success. Make sports an expression of your underlying spirit and purpose.

SURESHOT TECHNIQUE #6: INCLUDE THE SPIRITUAL PART OF YOURSELF IN YOUR ATHLETIC CAREER

Many highly accomplished athletes have sides we rarely hear about in the media. Once we know what they've done behind the scenes, it sometimes becomes clear that their passion and drive is not just in sport but also in their lifestyle and values.

The 15-time All-Star and World Series Champion baseball player Roberto Clemente was more than just an excellent batter.[90] He also knocked hearts out of the ballpark with his regular charity work in Latin America. Clemente represented a hero, both for baseball fans and Latinx people in need.

Eventually, Clemente would meet his end in a plane crash after a Nicaragua earthquake in 1972. His passing resounded with fans and people who felt his generosity up close. Today, he is a reminder that the unconditional acts of goodness we do off the field, court, or ring represent our character—and it might even positively affect our performance.

The Importance of the Spiritual Side

We all have a spiritual side. Whether we express it through actions, prayer, or a strong conviction in our values, it creates a sense of self-fulfillment. Our spirituality reminds us that life is not just about the physical rewards we gain. It's about creating a sense of peace and balance in all the facets of who we are: physical, emotional, social, and spiritual. When they all come together, we become self-actualized. That actually manifests itself in how we perform in our sport.[91]

To access your spiritual side, recognize that you hold a valuable place in the universe. It's your mission to carry out your duty and to make your wave in the world, however small.

SEEK A SPIRITUAL EXPERIENCE

Spirituality has fluid meaning—for some, it's tied to religion; for others, it's merely about connecting to your soul. Focusing on spiritual experiences doesn't have to be complex.

Some easy ways to access spirituality include meditation, yoga, reading, gratitude work, mindfulness, spending time in nature, and even simply helping others out.[92]

Meditation

Adding meditation to your routine can be beneficial for various reasons. In ancient cultures, athleticism and battle went side by side with meditation. In this case, meditation is a form of focused attention inward. It's about unplugging from the world and becoming centered within yourself.

Mediation can be a quick way to wind down if you're an athlete who's always on the go. Most importantly, it's one method to connect with your spiritual side, not just because it promotes mindfulness. One reason why Eastern philosophy promotes meditation is that it allows for a better distinction between the ego and your *real* self. You can disconnect from the useless thoughts that aren't actually coming from you. The real you is what some call your higher self or even awareness—it's your default state of being in which you access peace, self-possessed assurance for what is right for you. Deep down, you know what is wise and best, but your automatic thoughts can take hold of you.

To meditate, all you have to do is sit in a quiet, calm space and breathe for a few moments. Keep your breaths steady and slow, feeling tension roll off your body. Focus on being —just living, breathing, letting your body hold space. This is very different from being stuck in your head and tracking every endless circle of inner chatter.

Start with a few minutes. Meditation is a skill you can learn over time. Every week or so, tack on a minute, if that. However, that's not as important as doing it every day. Not only does mediation have tremendous implications for reducing chronic anxiety, but it also connects you to your higher self.

Yoga

As an ancient practice, yoga has been used as a physical exercise to access higher spiritual enlightenment. In Hindu culture, yoga poses affect the flow of chakra in the body, improving physical and mental health. For non-Hindus, yoga has been proven to increase a sense of positive well-being. Poses range from gentle stretches to more complicated movements that require intense mental control over the muscles. It also incorporates breathing techniques that affect the nervous system in different ways. When your life feels disorganized, practicing yoga gives you mental balance, stability, and clarity.

Reading

Sometimes, knowledge is what is missing on our journey to nourish our spiritual side. Reading, rather than consuming short-form content (videos, blogs, etc.), is one of the best ways to gain knowledge because it's an in-depth experience. When you read a book—particularly nonfiction, self-developmental, philosophical, or spiritual texts—you get to explore a topic thoroughly. That knowledge sinks into your mind better than someone offering advice or reading a sentence on the internet.

If you subscribe to a particular religion or spirituality, reading your relevant spiritual text bit by bit daily reminds you of your true purpose.

Practicing Gratitude

Being grateful every day unlocks a door in your brain to see more positivity. When it comes to spirituality, gratitude gives life more purpose. When you acknowledge and genuinely appreciate all your blessings, you feel you have a greater reason to live life to the fullest.[93]

Every morning, while you're still in bed, think of one thing that fills you with gratitude.[94] Don't just think about it, but really feel the positive emotion wash over you. Alternatively, you can create alarms once a day or a couple of times to remind you to stop and think of something you're grateful for. This helps you reset, especially if you're in the middle of a busy, stressful day.

Mindfulness

Practice mindfulness throughout the day by taking breathing breaks when you can, like between classes, before or after your sports practice, in transport between places, and so on. Taking breathing breaks is one of the best ways to add more mindfulness to your life.

Every time you stop living on autopilot, you have the opportunity to turn to your spiritual side—your true self. When you switch to mindfulness at any given moment, you stop doing and thinking automatically.

One easy mindful breathing exercise is:

1. Inhale for 4 seconds.
2. Hold your breath for 4 seconds.
3. Exhale for 4 seconds.
4. Repeat 4 times.

Nature

All human beings need to go back to their roots once in a while. Even in this highly technological world, we must nourish our souls by going back to nature regularly. Science shows that spending time outside, in the sun, on the grass, and around greenery increases feel-good hormones and reduces anxiety.[96]

Try scheduling a daily walk through a park, nature reserve, or around the greenest area near you. Perhaps you might lie on the grass and watch the clouds, or jog on a nearby trail through the woods. Spending time in nature grounds you and reminds you that your responsibilities are not as heavy and powerful as the earth and its miracles.

All of these activities don't take too long and can create significant shifts of positive change to your spiritual side. The question is: what is the connection between spirituality and sports?

Sports and Spirituality

Spirituality gives athletes strength in their field. On the flip side, sports allow you to channel your spiritual self. The physical moves you make are powered by your philosophy. If you invest time in your spiritual side, it can:

- Unlock personal development
- Help you feel connected to your community
- Rekindle a sense of inner purpose

Notice that so many athletes use their sport as a spiritual outlet. Many use their past pain to drive them through each match. Others use a hopeful future to keep them looking forward. Athletes connected to their spirituality use it to give them strength and determination. Spirituality and sports, when fused together, can make a sportsperson even more powerful, inspired, and unstoppable.

Being a champion takes soul. Some of it is skill, but a big part is about aligning the spirit with the body, pushing forward with a burning fire in the heart.

Take one of Michael Jordan's most exceptional moments.

It was 1992. An NBA Finals game was underhead—Chicago Bulls versus Portland. In the first half only, Michael Jordan had already shot six 3-pointers.

When asked how he did it, Jordan seemed not to know. It was like an out-of-body experience. He just sunk into a hyper-focused state of being that allowed him to make dunk after dunk. How? He didn't know. All he knew was *why*—he just had to win. In an effort to meet that purpose, Michael had a singular thought during the game—missing a shot was not an option.

The perfect balance of spirit and focus created a sense of peace that monks feel during a long meditation session. It's a calm stillness, a sense of taking your seat at the throne and commanding the body to move to your will. Driven by a purposeful spirit, you can access this flow state and do anything. Being in the zone or experiencing the flow state is a mind-body connection and synchronization. The two work together as one, leading to a sense of fulfillment.

Knowing who you are, soul-deep, and using it to strengthen you in the moments you need it most will build resilience. Your spirit solidifies *why* you're doing your sport. Now, it's time to get to work. Stack up your resilience by showing up stronger and better every day.

8

DAY-TO-DAY WINS

"Problems are not the problem; coping is the problem."

— VIRGINIA SATIR

D aily life is filled with gains and losses. You wake up early and start the day right—that's a gain. You mess up during practice and feel humiliated in front of everyone—that's a loss. The goal is not to increase your successes or reduce your failures. It's to *deal* with both properly. As Virginia Satir makes clear, how we cope with bad situations can make them worse.

Luckily, coping is something we can control. With aware-ness, effort, and repetition, we can switch our normal reaction to a more helpful response. The more we get the hang of healthier coping mechanisms, the better we can get through daily chaos.

Now it's time to combine what you've learned and integrate those lessons into small, daily steps.

SURESHOT TECHNIQUE #7: DO WHAT WORKS, EVERY DAY

The Stoics believed consistency was key—instead of doing a big thing at once, do a small thing consistently. Take things day by day, even if the day's achievements seem inconsequential. Anything can become a meaningful act if we choose.

In 2007, a sofa store in Charlestown, South Carolina, suffered a horrible fire.[90] Nine local firefighters passed away, one of them being the Summerville High School basketball coach. Naturally, the basketball team was heartbroken. This was their biggest loss—more important than any game they'd ever had.

To honor his memory, the team decided to put their all into the games, going all the way to the State Championships. They eventually won by a tiny margin, getting their key victory points in the game's last few moments. That win, they dedicated to their late coach.

The Summerville basketball team shows us an important example of making life events more meaningful. After all, humans will give meaning to everything and anything, whether they are doing it consciously or not. The team could have chosen to see the game as a sad event they won't get to share with their late coach. That mentality might have made winning harder; it's not very empowering.

Instead, they decided to share the game with their coach in their hearts. They dedicated it to his memory and even won because of how meaningful the purpose was. A simple game was now something they had to win for their own principles.

Find Greater Meaning in Your Daily Tasks

Nothing is only what it seems to be. Every task is perceived differently by different people. The good news is that you can attach whatever meaning you want to it.[93]

It's up to you to make your daily tasks meaningful, whether it's brushing your teeth or taking a history test. Everything in life has a purpose. When you are conscious of this fact, you can choose that purpose.

Connect everything you do to your big goals.[94] When you do, everything becomes a small win. For example, say your goal in life is to be a disciplined person. Perhaps you're inspired by diligent athletes and Navy SEALS who speak of amazing acts of self-control and strength. You can decide that doing your tasks properly, no matter how much interest you initially have in them, is one way of working toward yourself. What happens then? You become more motivated to conduct your entire life diligently. You start to take care of your chores, keep your room organized, and clean every dish after you eat. Over time, these mundane tasks become more meaningful.

It's up to you how much you want something to make a difference in your life. As for your athletic life, you can use your sport to further your greater purpose.

Ask yourself these questions:

- How can you connect your sport with your values and principles in life?
- How can you use your sport to make you a better person?
- Are your daily tasks making a difference in you, your life, or your athletic goal?

The meaning of life for you is whatever you want. Following your purpose is more important than chasing happiness. It transcends the self because your purpose allows you to do things according to your principles. Happiness fades, but purpose and meaningfulness lead to long-term positive impacts. Chasing the dream of becoming an Olympic athlete could be for fame or money, but these are temporary pleasures. Alternatively, you could chase it because your chosen purpose is to see how far you can surpass your limits. You might also choose to be an

Olympian to be recognized and spread the word about a cause that affects your community. The point is that material success is not the final stop. It's a stepping stone to achieving a greater aim.

Even before we get to that success, we ascribe meaning to the events along the way. Whenever an event occurs, you draw an inner conclusion that may aid or discourage you. If you fail, you might conclude that it means your goal is not meant to be. Instead, try interpreting failures as moments that prepared you to be even better. Failure is a lesson that allows us to hone our skills and prevents us from remaining complacent.

With this knowledge, you can choose what meaning to give the events in your life. The meaning of every situation depends on three things:[94]

1. Purpose
2. Coherence
3. Significance

Purpose refers to your aims and goals. What are you here for? What is your greater role in life?

Coherence is how you tie events together. We do this all the time naturally to create a narrative for what has happened in our life so far. Humans like to understand things through patterns and connections. Without coherence, we may feel that life is a purposeless series of random coincidences.

Coherence is how we fit a situation into the grand scheme of things when we try to make sense of everything later.

Significance is the strength of an event's meaning. Some people might focus more on certain events than others. A person's first soccer game loss might hit harder than their fiftieth loss.

Having a strong purpose that you paint into every task is advantageous. It pushes you to do things as well as you can, and it's also good for growing your character. Having a clear purpose in life improves well-being and life contentment. It increases resilience because we care more about the things we do and therefore have more energy to resist giving up. It improves self-esteem and reduces the risk of depression.

Reflect on how you want to live. This is not regarding material items, like what car or house you want. It's about what you imagine your ideal lifestyle is. One's idea might include plenty of family time, daily morning runs, and volunteering once a week. A martial arts lover might prefer a life full of various classes to explore the world's many forms of fighting. Life could also look like working a job you love so that you hardly feel like you're working.

Use the following techniques and tools to discover your purpose and make life more meaningful:

- **Chase discipline:** Living with purpose, regardless of your goal, is living with discipline. An undisciplined human is a human without reason or rhyme. Even if you don't know what your life goal is, start building your self-control, self-empowerment, physical and mental energy, and emotional mastery. Start practicing conscious communication and eloquence, as well as proper interpersonal communication skills. These things will help you fulfill your potential and reach your goals.

- **Make life enjoyable:** You already have things that bring you joy in life, and it's those things that can clue you in on your purpose. Focus more on them by loving your loved ones as best as possible and spending time with people you care about.

- **Pursue an interest or hobby:** Try something you've always wanted to do but were never given a chance. A new hobby will provide a healthy challenge and open doors for you.

- **Reconsider how you think about insecurities:** Are you thinking constantly about your shortcomings? If your insecurities are going in circles in your mind with no resolution, it's time to stop. It's a waste of time. Instead, focus only on what you can change or improve. If it's out of your control, that negative self-talk is useless.

- **Become a lifelong learner:** The pursuit of knowledge is a worthy life purpose. Even if it's not your main goal, make it your lifelong journey to always keep learning.

Stop and Assess

Is what you're doing right now, today, pushing you forward? Or is it pulling you back?

Check your perspective. What is the narrative tying your story together? See the big picture of your small moment. Where does it lie in your story? Stopping and assessing is a way of resetting yourself. It allows you to give feedback on whether your current trajectory is pointed to your goal.

Don't look at the stuff in your way. Look at the path winding around and between the obstacles. Always expect problems and failures. Some people go as far as to welcome them. After all, if problems happen anyway, we may as well greet them with open arms. This mindset is one step up from acceptance.

Cultivate Gratitude

Gratitude has a ton of scientific benefits on physical and mental health.[97] Spiritually, gratitude raises your energy. Whether you believe it or not, you attract what you give out (for the most part). Make gratitude a daily non-negotiable. Be grateful for what is working and what is teaching you a lesson. Keep focused on those positive blessings.[98, 99]

Keep Life Simple

We already know complexity is bad. This also goes for increasing your day-to-day wins. Reduce your material possessions, organize and cut down on unimportant time commitments, and even simplify your words.[100] When it comes to diet, reduce complexity by having a set list of daily meals.[101]

Discover Your True North

Sometimes, what can help you uncover your purpose or your true north is seeing what mottos resonate with you.[102] A motto is like an affirmation, one that defines who you are and what you believe in. Choose one of them to guide you or make up your own.

Here are some examples of famous mottos:[103]

- "Just do it."
- "Keep calm and keep going."
- "You only live once."
- "Keep your eyes on the prize."
- "Today is another day."
- "Carpe diem (seize the day)."
- "I am unstoppable."
- "Anything is possible."

A personal motto provides a repetitive reminder to keep you sticking to goals, keeping up the image you want to portray, and providing calm in stressful moments.

Try This: Create your personal motto, using inspiration from mottos or quotes that strike you as important.

Make a list of what you need to declutter in your life.

Mental strength and resilience are not about being able to push a mountain. It's about the small, consistent wins. Moving each stone one by one to clear the road. It's in those small habits that you pave your way to success.

Being mentally strong is also about accepting and letting go. All athletes, at some point, must practice trusting self-mastery like a Buddhist monk.

9

THE ZEN ATHLETE

"Surfing soothes me, it's always been a kind of Zen experience for me. The ocean is so magnificent, peaceful, and awesome. The rest of the world disappears for me when I'm on a wave."

— PAUL WALKER

Being an athlete doesn't require you to push and try hard all the time. Massive action and taking charge are key components of success. However, balance is always beneficial. In this case, it's important to practice the art of acceptance.

Acceptance is not apathy. It's not giving up; on the contrary, it's a power move. All it means is you remain calm and at peace with whatever obstacles life brings. If you are struggling to hone a skill in your sport, accepting that struggle can be more helpful than rejecting its existence.

However, acceptance is not easy. You must navigate a fine line between acknowledgment and learned helplessness.

- Acknowledgment: I accept that I am not good at this right now. That does not mean I will not become better.
- Learned helplessness: I am not good at this right now, which means I'll never be good. I may as well give up now.

When you learn to accept reality, no matter how harsh it is, it becomes easier to cope and move on quickly. This is essential to growing your resilience. The warriors who lose their wits lose the war on the battlefield. Letting anxiety grow will not make you run faster on the track.

Accessing that Zen state, just as Paul Walker did while surfing, opens up the opportunity for honed calm and focus that lead to success.

SURESHOT TECHNIQUE #8: TO WIN, STAY CALM, FOCUSED, AND COOL

Phil Jackson is one of the most successful basketball coaches nationally.[104] Because of him, the Chicago Bulls and Los Angeles Lakers went beyond any goal thought possible. Phil helped his teams score more championships than anyone else, and there's a big reason why.

It wasn't his teaching methods, his way of selecting the right players, or even his coaching skill. A lot of it was due to his mentality. Phil Jackson based all of his coaching methods on values. His teaching style was embedded with value-based language that inspired, not just instructed. He didn't just tell his players what to do; he focused on why.

Most coaches, to motivate their team, don't do it the right way. Half of them might pump their team up with ego-driven affirmations that are shallow and short-lived. They may say stuff like "We're the champions! The best of the best! Let's show them what we've got!" The other half might use fear-based tactics like "Do you want to be known as the losers?!" and "We poured sweat, blood, and tears into this, so don't let yourself regret it!" Both tactics can be motivating, but only for a short time because they are surface-level.

Instead, Phil told his team to remember why they were doing it. While it's not as loud or pumped up, this approach can get through to our core because it's personally meaningful.

People never remember what happens. They remember what events *mean* to them.

We are all incredibly driven by purpose. How many times has a high school student asked their math teacher, "Why do we need this? It's not like we're ever going to use it." Without a valid, personally important reason to do something, doing it feels useless and uninspiring. However, if those high school students were to see the bigger picture, they might realize that math knowledge builds up to more advanced studies that help to enter societally important careers that can give them better future lives. This is just one example— anyone can choose what makes anything meaningful to them. No matter why, as long as it's valuable and tied to your foundational purpose or goal, it works. It fuels you for the long term.

On the other hand, acting like many essential tasks are meaningless or useless is delusional. Saying something has no purpose to yourself or, in general, is a result of fear. You see the task as challenging, so you use its meaninglessness as an excuse. Yet, if you were to attach a purpose to it, you might have become strong enough to take the challenge on. It's a choice, and that choice is to avoid problems and avoid reality.

Resisting Reality

Refusing to see reality is like drinking poison. Tiny doses of poison will blur your perception over time, leaving you blind to what you really need to see. Seeing life's problems head-on allows you to find potential solutions. At the very least, accepting them reduces psychological distress. Being resilient is not about ignoring the pain; it's about facing that pain anyway and going through it with resolve.

Moreover, ignoring reality leads to an inability to let go of control. Athletes are not meant to be control freaks. They must work fluidly with what they have. However, when you can't accept a certain outcome like, say, losing a game, it may lead to unsavory action. You might do whatever it takes to win and even resort to unethical actions. For instance, you might lower yourself to cheating, forcing an outcome, lying, or manipulating—none of which should be a part of an athlete's values. Or you might have an angry outburst revealing a lack of good sportsmanship. Nothing makes a person lose the respect of others more than being a sore loser.

Resisting that what happens in life is not power. It comes from fear. As you've read so far, athletes must learn to capture and manage their fear, not let it overpower them.

What You Resist Persists

When you resist something, it's likely to follow you around.[105] Opposites attract, after all. It's because you are focusing more on what you do not want. Anytime you are afraid of an outcome, even though you think you are ignoring it, you are actually giving it more power. The problem will stay or continually arise in your life. This is because you are putting so much mental (and maybe physical) energy into avoiding it.

Resisting results from an unwillingness to deal with negative experiences. Many falsely assume that ignoring the bad stuff, like fear, discomfort, and pain, will lead to happiness.[106] However, happiness is not found in the comfort zone. It's found more in learning to manage stress and difficulty. Protecting yourself will never lead to thriving.

That's why sports can be good for everyone and anyone. While sports do involve physical risks, they also present opportunities to grow in the face of stress, pressure, and fear. Doing so in a controlled situation prepares you for life's challenges too.

Moreover, resisting comes from not resolving emotions. If you are afraid of facing something, avoiding it doesn't make the fear disappear. You get attached to the fear and other unresolved feelings. As we learned before, feelings are messages. You should act on them consciously, allowing you to process or solve them. Left unsolved, they stick around. As Carl Jung once said, what you resist persists and even grows.[107]

The problem with this is that the rejection of reality takes energy. You may think it's useless to waste energy on facing something you don't want to do anyway. I invite you to change your perspective. Unresolved emotions will continue to be heavy on the mind and bubble up again and again. Trying to keep it in will take more out of you in the long run.

Instead, try tackling life like this: to get what you want, want what you get. This dissolves all resistance. The mentality is a general acceptance of all that comes your way. Imagine how strong you become when you love the result, no matter what happens. Avoidance allows the problem to continue, and you may never face it if you act like it doesn't exist. Meanwhile, accepting what is true puts you in a mindful place where you can change and improve. Acceptance is not a defeat; it's a strength.

Accept and welcome anything that comes your way. It's the smart thing, the purposeful thing, and it saves time, money, and energy.

THE ZEN APPROACH

The Zen philosophy is a way of life that Zen Buddhist monks practice.[108] The philosophy aims to simplify everything: mind, body, and soul. The good news is that you don't have to be a monk to benefit from a Zen lifestyle.

Certain principles can be applied, such as living simply. Get rid of unnecessary and unimportant things to focus on the important ones. Some things are necessary, and some are not. A good practice for athletes is to try to live with less than they usually do as an extra challenge.

Meditate during mundane tasks like cleaning and cooking. Embedding mindfulness in your everyday life, especially for boring tasks, helps you concentrate better. You can do them slowly and with full focus. Alternatively, you can meditate while sitting, running, working out, etc. Create a routine with designated times for rituals—rituals and routines help you stay on a system. To be more Zenlike, follow these main principles.[109]

Ego Denial

Denying the ego means no longer identifying with your surface-level thoughts. These thoughts often start with "I," like "I am an athlete" or "I am a student." When it comes to labels, identities, status, position, jobs, or other ways of describing ourselves, that makes up our ego. Identifying with the ego means we attach ourselves to every thought we have. If we think, "I'm such a failure," our thoughts resound as true. The ego is about being what you have. To deny the ego is to simply *be*.

To separate yourself from the ego or your false sense of self, consider who you would be without the things in your life— your sport, your school identity, your family, your culture, your hobbies and interests, your socioeconomic status, your gender identity, etc. Who are you in essence? What if you lost any of those things overnight?

If you feel you would be less without those things, it means you identify with the ego. That means you have open points of weakness that you must take care of. When you can reach a point where your ego is not as powerful, you will achieve greater mental toughness. True power is feeling undefeated, even when you are stripped of everything you have.

Interconnectedness

One of the foundational beliefs in Zen Buddhism is that everything is interdependent. No one exists in a vacuum. One individual is connected to another in some way, physically or energetically. We are also connected to the ground, plants, animals, nature, and the universe. With this philosophy, we can learn to think beyond ourselves. We can see greater value in being of service to others for more selfless reasons.

Attachment Is Suffering

Attachment is the source of all human suffering. What exactly is attachment? It is when you stubbornly hold on to things in this physical world, be it a thing, person, experience, or idea.

Attachment is suffering because you are not guaranteed permanent possession of these things. Humans die or leave; you are not entitled to any opportunity, money, job, or place in life, even if you work hard for it.

This is not to say that you should isolate yourself, give up on your sport, or stop trying in life. Attachment has its extremes. For instance, you can aim to win a championship game. However, you should not be so obsessed with winning that you start neglecting other aspects, including your health —an example of an unhealthy attachment. In this case, you are attached to a specific outcome, and the attachment is holding you back more than it is helping.

If you want to know whether it's time to detach yourself from something, see if it's causing you more pain than peace.

Human Perception Is Flawed

Our perception of reality is subjective, which means it is undoubtedly imperfect. We often live with the idea that because something is how we think it is, that's how it is. If this is how we feel, then it must be true. Recognizing that human perception is inherently flawed gives us greater wisdom. It allows us to question our minds and offers a different perspective of looking at things.

HOW TO PRACTICE ACCEPTANCE IN REAL LIFE

Practicing acceptance is key to nurturing mental toughness. Undeniably, you will fall into circumstances you don't like. When you are attached to a specific outcome, you cannot accept anything but that outcome. The Stoic philosophers used to say something along the lines of, "Don't wish for what you want to happen, wish for things to happen as they do."

The mentality of acceptance prevents you from being attached to things that might make you suffer more than you should. As such, acceptance is synonymous with non-attachment.

According to LPC Aaron Dutil, "Not being completely attached to material objects can help people build a resilient mindset."[110] Unhealthy attachment looks like stressing about things out of your control. You might be burdened by internal stress or guilt or resentment. It's influenced negatively by anything that affects your mental focus, like rumination, hard feelings, hard situations, and external factors about which you can't do anything.

Learning to detach yourself is a skill that has to do with mindfulness. Therapy like Cognitive Behavioral Therapy (CBT) includes concepts like being aware of thoughts, emotions, and behavior that are not serving you and coming to a place where you can consciously choose to step back from it. Practicing non-attachment looks like choosing how you respond to things out of your control. It helps clear your mind, tame your thoughts, and increase self-compassion.

Practicing non-attachment will require internal work.[109] Most of the stuff we worry about and pour our strength into are things we can't change. For example, you might encounter a rude insult, hurtful actions, or loss of an opportunity. As unpleasant as these things are, we can learn not to let losses define us.

The goal of non-attachment is not to eliminate fear, sadness, or strong emotions. Rather, it's to protect yourself from such emotions overwhelming you. The same applies to material items or ego-driven achievements like fame, money, and success. You can, of course, have goals to attain these material achievements, but your non-attachment will give you a sense of freedom: Without them, you'll still be okay; and this will give you strength.

Of course, all of this is not easy. The more you practice, the better you can become at distancing yourself from the current situation in a way that allows you to have more clarity in your choice.

HOW TO LET GO OF MISTAKES

Whether you got too arrogant and neglected your training or let social pressure lead you to ignore your responsibilities, we all make mistakes at one point or other.

Forgive Yourself and Others

Forgiveness is not just about making yourself feel better; it's a form of processing and letting go of pent-up resentment toward yourself and others. Parents, colleagues, or friends may have hurt you, but choosing not to forgive them will continue to hurt you, even after they have moved on.

Forgiveness is a decision to release resentment and thoughts of getting back at someone. The more you forgive, the better your life gets. Believe it or not, unforgiveness can destroy mental and physical health. Depression, anxiety, high blood pressure, and a weak immune system can all stem from clutching to moments you've been wronged that you cannot seem to forget.

Of course, you are entitled to feel the pain of betrayal or sadness. However, holding a grudge is not rational. It will not help you with anything in life, neither your sport nor your relationships. You might have a lot of baggage of unforgiven deeds going into new friendships. You can become stuck in the past. In the end, the person that gets hurt is you.

Self-forgiveness is even harder to do sometimes. You are the one doing the forgiving, and you might be harsher than others toward yourself.

How to forgive yourself and others?

1. Ask why you or they might have behaved that way.
2. Reflect on yourself and if you hurt others (or yourself).
3. Journal or meditate on your thought process with the intention of forgiveness.
4. Forgiveness is a process. You may need to forgive someone else or yourself several times, maybe even daily.

Know that reconciliation is not always necessary. Forgiveness is not about giving the other person another chance; it's about changing your life.[111]

If you need forgiveness, acknowledge the wrongs and how they affected others. If truly sorry, apologize without making excuses.

Look for the Lesson and Move On

Feel your feelings without judgment. Don't let yourself accept automatic negative thoughts that make things seem permanent or unsolvable; instead, challenge those thoughts. Think about how you responded to a situation in the past that was stressful or challenging. Did the response make you feel better or worse? Was it a response, or did you react rashly? This is a conscious reflection of the past that allows you to actually learn. Experience is a lesson, but if you try to erase and ignore the past or, on the flip side, ruminate over it every day, you won't learn anything.[112]

Rumination manifests from not accepting the past. You want to control how the past turned out, so you keep obsessing over it and rehashing it mentally in a subconscious effort to change it but, as we all know, you can't change the past. Instead, you're wasting your time in the present instead of making actual changes now. As C.S. Lewis said, "You can't go back and change the beginning, but you can start where you are and change the ending."

Trying to forget the past doesn't work either. It's just avoidance that leads to not learning anything valuable. You might continue cultivating the same self-defeating patterns again and again, wondering what's wrong.

Non-acceptance typically leads to more problems. Try reflecting on your biggest mistakes in a journal or meditation.[113] Ask yourself difficult questions.

- What about this mistake is so meaningful to me?
- What led me to make this mistake?
- How would I have acted differently?
- What can I do now to avoid making this mistake again?
- What responses can I have ready in the future in case this situation arises again?

These questions are focused on processing and breaking down the events leading up to your mistake while also exploring potential solutions.

Leave the Past Behind You

The past no longer exists. Do not forget it but leave it and let it go. Don't let old mistakes hold you back. Thinking about them over and over is neither a way of forgiveness, nor is punishing yourself for it. If it's not helping you improve your present or future, it's unnecessary complexity.[114]

After learning what you need to learn, it's time to focus on the present and what you're doing now. Are you at risk of making the same mistake? If you stay stuck in the past, you'll just create more things to regret.

Keep in mind the following mantras to keep your head forward and your demons behind you:

- "It is what it is."
- "Nothing to be done about it."
- "Don't look back."
- "The present changes the past."

As Søren Kierkegaard once said, "Life can only be understood backwards; but it must be lived forwards."

Try this: List what parts of your life have a lot of resistance for you. Thinking of what you know now about acceptance, is there another strategy to deal with it? Is there a challenge you are avoiding or an outcome that terrifies you? Consider how accepting it might change the situation for you.[115]

The good thing about all this is that you're not the only one who has undergone these struggles. Many athletes before have faced the same challenges as you. With many of the principles in this book, they have been able to achieve the success they dreamed of. Find inspiration in their stories to see how mentality can really be a game-changer.

10

SUCCESS IN REAL TIME

"To all the other dreamers out there, don't ever stop or let the world's negativity disenchant you or your spirit. If you surround yourself with love and the right people, anything is possible."

— ADAM GREEN

I f you put your mind to it, anything is possible. The proof of that is in the multitudes of athletes' stories out there. Seeing another person like you get to where you want to be and how they did it is truly inspiring. It's the nudge you need to embark on a journey of building resilience in sports and beyond.

SURESHOT TECHNIQUE #9: GET INSPIRED AND STAY INSPIRED

The following stories can give you extra strength and ammunition to help you achieve your athletic dream.[118] Come back to this whenever you need the conviction to keep going.

David Sills

From the age of 9, David Sills' dad recognized his son's amazing skill at quarterbacking.[116] He was so good that he got an offer from the University of Santa Monica team for the Trojans at age 13. Yet, despite being a young prodigy, David didn't forget or neglect his work ethic. He remained laser-focused on his goal, never stopping because he thought he was good enough.

However, things didn't go as planned. David eventually lost the offer he was initially offered. He tried his hardest to fulfill his quarterback dreams. Yet no offers came.

David got the message. He was ready to move on.

The lesson here? Never regret the honorable act of trying to do something to the best of your ability before giving up. Moreover, don't be afraid to move on if it's not working out; there's no shame in that.

David switched his single-minded determination to becoming the best receiver, and indeed, he did become the best after only a year. Perhaps it wasn't his natural talent that made David special, but rather his continued hard work and adaptability.

Freddy Adu

At age 14, soccer player Freddy Adu showed clear promise. He was one of the most talented players, winning his DC United team during the 2004 MLS Cup. Imagine being offered a pro contract at such a young age!

Unfortunately, because he was so young, his playing time was less than it would have been for an adult player. This was for the sake of his growth and development. Despite this, Freddy continued excelling throughout his life until he began to play professionally by 24 years old.

Freddy's story shows us that age doesn't matter.

Wayne Gretzky

In 1979, Wayne was only 19 years old when he joined the Edmonton Oilers hockey team. Soon after, he helped the team win the Hart Memorial Trophy, a highly acclaimed award in the sport of Hockey. He would go on to win eight of those trophies all in a row, a notable streak for someone so young.

Interestingly, it's not that Wayne was particularly ambitious. In reality, he just pursued what he wanted. He truly enjoyed skating, going as far as doing so for 8 hours a day at just 6 years old. That enjoyment stuck with him, perhaps unintentionally making him the best at what he did. Even after gaining fame for his astounding plays, he was immune. He preferred to be treated like any normal teenager/young adult by his teammates and the media. In other words, it's evident that Wayne found success simply by following his true north.

Gretzky has now won the title "The Great One" for getting more points at his age than anyone else in hockey history.

Spencer Wilson

Spectacular athletes are able to channel an unchangeable life pain into something positive. Things like illness and death are parts of life we cannot ignore. While they can fill us with grief, that grief can be transformed into inspirational action.

That is exactly what teenager Spencer Wilson did.

As a student at Bishop McGuinness Catholic High School, he was involved in the Dedication Game, an event in which basketball players play for the sake of an important person in their life. Who did Spencer choose? He dedicated the game to a dear friend who had passed away a year before from cancer. The two bonded over shared difficulty—they met when Spencer himself was battling cancer. Three years ago, doctors told Spencer he had half a year of life left. However, he survived, not once, but twice. Unfortunately, his friend, Josh Rominger, did not, and Spencer used this opportunity to dedicate the game to him.

Spencer's story highlights what all athletes should strive to do: make the game or the competition about something greater than yourself. When the goal goes beyond the win or the medal, you are sure to put your heart and soul into your sport.

Melinda Harrison

Right now, it may feel like your sport is everything. On the flip side, you may feel pressured by the idea that your future is limited or constrained by your sport. What happens after you've met all your goals? Even worse, what happens if you don't achieve the goal you've been working toward for most of your life, like making a college team or getting into a prestigious academy?

Melinda's story is an example of flexibility.[117]

As a swimmer, Melina was single-minded. Her goal was to get to the Olympics, and every part of her day was structured with that aim in mind. She trained full-time and was an Olympian before graduating college. She was an All-American and Silver Medalist at NCAA.

When she accomplished her goals, she was excited for the next step in her life.

If you're a young athlete, you may know this feeling well. Some want to pour everything into their sport, be the best they can, and then upon succeeding in all of their dreams, move on to the next project, be it studying something they've always wanted or getting their dream job if they weren't an athlete. Unfortunately, it's hard to juggle between sports versus other things at this stage in life. Becoming a successful athlete requires full-time commitment and effort, with little time to invest in studies or careers. As such, it's hard not to think of yourself as anything but an athlete since every minute of your day revolves around it.

Life never goes as we expect. We know this book is about creating a strong mental attitude that leads you to success in your athletic career. We can't talk about mental toughness without facing the elephant in the room . . . what if you don't succeed? What if you don't make it to the team, the nationals, the championships, or the Olympics? What if it ends too early after you've had an incredible winning streak? What if your purpose fizzles out, and you find that your successes are no longer driving you? To be resilient, you must be prepared to exercise flexibility in your life goals when things change. You must be prepared to create a new life that doesn't revolve around your sport.

Melinda learned this the hard way. When she met her milestones, she didn't realize how hard it would be to shift her focus from her sport to something else. She forgot how it felt to live a normal life and experienced some unexpected side effects:

1. Losing recognition: You might get used to cheers and celebrations from the audience or your friends and

family. That external validation can be almost addictive. The true test of mental toughness would be during transitioning. When all the positive things are about sports, how do you react when that phase is over? Will you remain strong and weather it by focusing on internal validation, wholeness, resiliency, and discipline, using what you learned in sports?

2. Mental health effects: Transition can be scary, sad, or stressful. Melinda learned that focusing on mental health is crucial when making the transition.

3. Taking responsibility may be difficult for athletes who have been used to others structuring their routine for them, be it their coach or parents. What will you do to maintain a consistent regimen without practices, meets, and games? This is another hard part of being an athlete. Maybe your discipline depended on time constraints and routine, but it doesn't mean you're not strong or make those scheduling decisions yourself to allow your self-discipline to flourish. Remember to navigate the transition with a cool responsibility. Try not to fall into deleterious habits like staying out too late or waking up whenever or eating anything just because you can.

Now, Melinda is a professional certified executive coach with experience in discovering and realizing goals. She's helping other people and athletes know where to go next. Ever since she went from Olympian to businesswoman, she knows how to teach others to bounce from one goal to the next.

Melinda's story is one of success, both in sports and otherwise. Most importantly, it teaches us to be an athlete in life, not just in sports.

Mike Tyson

As a teenager, Mike Tyson was already a prolific boxer. He was ruthless in every match. By age 18, Mike had a streak of knockouts. By the time he made his professional debut, he had won against Hector Mercedes with a knockout in the first round. He was the youngest boxer to win World Boxing Champion heavyweight titles at age 20. The year he became champion, 1986, was the year right after his trainer and legal guardian died. His death provided Mike with more reason to be a champion.

It's not until later in his career that we understand why Mike was so set on being the most dangerous boxer. To this day, he talks about his past and where he came from—it wasn't an easy childhood with a house, a family, and a picket fence. It's clear that Mike drew his viciousness from his dark past, where he had to rely on himself.

Today, Mike Tyson is truly an inspiration, not just for his early success but also for his undeniable wisdom. Unlike others, he hasn't been afraid to admit his faults and past mistakes. Tyson has left us with many deep, resonant quotes to remember when going through our own struggles. For instance, he famously said, "Self-discipline is doing what you hate, but doing it like you love it."

Mary Lou Retton

In the 1980s, there emerged a world-class female gymnast. This gymnast was only 16 years old when she achieved this title. Mary Lou Retton was a remarkable American gymnast who underwent and won the US nationals and the US Olympic trials, all before the age of 18.

Unfortunately, tragedy hit in 1984 when she had to get operated on her knee due to an injury. She didn't want to miss her chance to perform at the Olympics, so she managed to get the surgery done before the Olympics.

That year, the Olympics were held on US soil in Los Angeles. It's good that she made it because Mary Lou shocked the crowd and the judges. She received consecutive perfect scores of 10 during the floor exercise and won one of the five gold medals. That year, she appeared in Sports Illustrated as their "Sportswoman of the Year."

These stories show us that age doesn't matter. Countless young athletes, teenagers, and young adults have achieved mind-blowing results. Knowing their stories can motivate you and inspire you to try your best. Gaining inspiration from similar people who you aspire to be builds faith in your potential.

FINAL WORDS

*"You have survived 100% of everything in your life so far . . .
There's a good chance you'll survive whatever is next."*

— UNKNOWN

Resilience is not something you can buy. It is accessible to anyone, so long as you work toward building it as a skill. It is a valuable skill that makes you the king of your mind, the master of your emotions.

Most importantly, resilience will keep you going even in the most challenging moments.

All athletes undergo challenges. From physiological stressors to emotional issues and physical obstacles to competition, many factors affect their performance. Injuries, slumps, pressure, and life conflicts are some examples of their stressors.

Many people wrongly assume resilience is a talent or an inherent trait. Resilience is not something one is born with. Research has proven that anyone can develop and nurture skills that contribute to overall resilience. It's a muscle that grows stronger with each use. You are working that muscle every time you stumble and get back up. Next time you fall, you spring up much faster, with more determination and motivation to succeed.

Peak resilience is when failure fuels you more than success.

You can become resilient by adopting the right mindset and learning specific coping strategies to navigate challenges. Such strategies will create a formidable mind that can withstand injuries and setbacks in athletic performance. It can give you unshakeable confidence, determination, and self-esteem so that no external challenge affects how you feel about yourself.

In sports, you can see the physical effects of resilience. Use your athletic life as an opportunity to practice resiliency, and it will also appear in other areas of life. Of course, being mentally tough will undoubtedly improve your performance.

Often, what sets athletes apart is not the hours of work they put in, the coach they have, or the money they have; it is about their minds of steel and iron will.

As a young athlete, you want to be a world-class winner. However, the irony is: if you want to be a star in your sport, you have to be in this for yourself—not for the world.

What that means is that the most important skills are goal-setting, purpose-defining, and passion-burning. To be like the famous athletes that inspire, you must follow these techniques to build resilience.

THE 9 SURESHOT TECHNIQUES TO INCREASE RESILIENCE & FORGE AN INVINCIBLE MINDSET

#1: Have a Clear Direction in Life: Without direction, you will be fumbling all over the place. To become an excellent athlete, you must take aim. After you shoot the first arrow, you can recalibrate your aim, but always start with a clear direction.

#2: Get Clear on What Is Holding You Back: Many athletes wonder what's wrong in their lives. Why aren't they progressing? If this is you, consider what self-defeating habits may be getting in your way. Perhaps it's the people in your life, the unhealthy sleep schedule or diet, or even your negative self-talk. It's time to cut that all out to reduce any obstacles holding you back.

#3: Know What Is Good for You: Anything that gives you a boost, any skill or talent you have, needs to be maximized. Working at your fullest potential requires knowing what is good for you and your physical and mental well-being. You are responsible for ensuring your body and mind are thriving and ready to take on anything.

#4: Master Your Mind and Mindset: Your mind is your greatest asset. When your body stops working, your mind will keep on going. It's important to increase your power over it and master your mindset. Shift your perspective, and life will shift to meet your requests.

#5: Master Your Emotions and Use Their Energy to Drive You Forward: Mental toughness requires managing your emotions. Being the master of your feelings allows you to channel them into energy. Whether it's negative emotion driving you or positive emotion beckoning you forward, you can take advantage of it.

#6: Include the Spiritual Part of Yourself in Your Athletic Career: Sports and spirit are inseparable. Young athletes can use this to their advantage. The more care and effort you put into your spiritual side—be it through religious prayer or peaceful meditation, the greater your fuel for carrying out your goal.

#7: Do What Works, Every Day: Daily, consistent, and persistent actions are more important than massive one-time wins. Figure out what works for you and keep at it. As for what doesn't work, you have already learned to shift your perspective and think outside the box. Every little task can be a stepping stone to your goal if you choose.

#8: To Win, Stay Calm, Focused, and Cool: Tough athletes remain unruffled. Trouble and challenge don't sway them. They stay zeroed in on the task at hand without being distracted by high emotion. The key to this is not apathy but accepting the way things are in the world.

#9: Get Inspired and Stay Inspired: Anything is possible as long as you believe in it. To stoke your belief and keep the fire of your passion burning, use inspiration from fellow athletes. Look to stories of young sportspersons just like you who defied the odds. Read up on some amazing feats young athletes have accomplished, like beating records or using their sports as a means to a greater end.

Remember that people with high resilience have the following characteristics:

1. Awareness
2. Self-control
3. Emotional management
4. Determination
5. Flexibility

To increase resilience, focus on these five things (5Cs): Confidence, Competence, Commitment, Connection to others, and Communication. Increasing any of these factors will massively increase your ability to endure hardships. These tenets are evident in the tips provided in this book. If you follow each step and implement even a few of the tools available, you'll find yourself growing stronger day by day.

Train your physical as well as your mental muscles because while our body's strength is capped, our minds are limitless.

FREE GOODWILL

Everyone has their personal thing that may build them up. However, there are also general things we all would be better off doing. Some things that would be recommended for everyone are: learning to do things selflessly, giving to others without expecting a reward or validation, and thinking about the world's interconnectedness.

Think about it. You're not the only one going through what you're going through. Otherwise, there wouldn't be a whole book written about it!

The more you meditate on the fact that you're not alone, the easier it is to be stronger. Pondering the world outside of ourselves helps us see that our problem is just a speck in the universe. It also helps us see others more compassionately, as opposed to viewing the world as a race to the finish line.

A mentally tough athlete or person will jump at the chance to give to another or help someone who used to struggle like them. Once you have more wisdom than you started with, you will better understand your past self and the people in your position.

Even more, you would welcome the opportunity to guide them to important knowledge in any way possible.

Luckily, there is a way that many don't even think about. There is at least a small action or word for everything that can get the ball rolling. In the case of helping other athletes eager to become more resilient, leaving a review can actually make a huge impact.

So many young athletes are spinning their wheels, working harder than ever. Yet they wonder why they don't feel fulfilled. Why every small failure makes them feel like giving up? They don't understand how their so-called passion could run out of steam so quickly. Or how it's possible to balance their sports goals with their social life.

Our mission with this book is to reach those just like you. If you could, please take a few seconds to leave an honest review of this book that mirrors the amount of value you've received. Your review will help struggling athletes find this resource and improve their mental and physical prowess.

REFERENCES

1. The Newsmen. 2021. "The incredible success story of Michael Jordan." Accessed October 27, 2022. https://thenewsmen.co.in/high-flyers/the-incredible-success-story-of-michael-jordan/44895

2. Raglin, John S. "Psychological Factors in Sport Performance." Sports Medicine 31, no. 12 (2001): 875–90. https://doi.org/10.2165/00007256-200131120-00004

3. Coolaboo. n.d. "Ancient Greek Sport Facts for Kids." Accessed September 30, 2022. https://www.coolaboo.com/world-history/ancient-greece/ancient-greek-sport/

4. Lambert, Tim. n.d. "A History of Sport." Local Histories. Accessed September 30, 2022. https://localhistories.org/a-history-of-sport/

5. LSU Online. n.d. "What Is the Role of Sports in Society?" NowComment. Accessed November 3, 2022. https://nowcomment.com/documents/97820

6. Gorcey, Ryan. n.d. "How Soccer Stopped The Great War | News, Scores, Highlights, Stats, and Rumors." Bleacher Report. Accessed September 30, 2022. https://bleacherreport.com/articles/96702-how-soccer-stopped-the-great-war

7. Cohn, Patrick. 2020. "Do Kids Feel like Sports is a Job?" Youth Sports Psychology. https://www.youthsportspsychology.com/youth_sports_psychology_blog/do-your-kids-feel-like-sports-is-a-job/

8. Ghildiyal, Rakesh. n.d. "Role of Sports in the Development of an Individual and Role of Psychology in Sports." NCBI. Accessed

October 27, 2022. https://www.ncbi.nlm.nih.gov/pmc/articles/
PMC4381313/

9. Abbott, Mara. n.d. "The Real Story on Authentic Goals--by Mara
    Abbott." Carmichael Training Systems. Accessed September 30,
    2022. https://trainright.com/real-story-authentic-goals-mara-
    abbott/

10. Whittlestone, Jess. 2014. "How Useful is Identity?" Jess
    Whittlestone. Accessed October 27, 2022. https://jesswhittlestone.
    com/blog/2014/4/19/how-useful-is-identity

11. Williams, Joanna L. 2018. "Adolescent Identity Development: What
    to Expect in Teens." Center for Parent and Teen Communication.
    Accessed October 27, 2022. https://parentandteen.com/
    developing-adolescent-identity/

12. Songco, Christine. n.d. "A list of common likes and dislikes to
    increase self-awareness." Third Bliss. Accessed October 27, 2022.
    https://thirdbliss.com/list-of-likes-and-dislikes/

13. Mind Tools Content Team. n.d. "What Are Your Values?" Mind
    Tools. Accessed October 27, 2022. https://www.mindtools.com/
    pages/article/newTED_85.htm

14. Raypole, Crystal. 2020. "Sense of Self: What It Is and How to Build
    It." Healthline. https://www.healthline.com/health/sense-of-self

15. Griffin, Trudi, and Stanley, Meghan. n.d. "How to Know Who You
    Are: 14 Steps (with Pictures)." wikiHow. Accessed October 27, 2022.
    https://www.wikihow.com/Know-Who-You-Are

16. Funk, Christine. 2015. "Maximize Your Strengths and Become Your
    Own Superhero." Bookboon. https://bookboon.com/blog/2015/
    11/be-your-own-superhero-maximize-your-strengths/

17. Michael, Jonathan. n.d. "How to Identify Your Strengths and Weaknesses." Bplans Blog. Accessed October 27, 2022. https://articles.bplans.com/how-to-identify-your-strengths-and-weaknesses/

18. Zetlin, Minda. 2015. "How the Most Effective Leaders Turn Weaknesses Into Strengths." Inc. Magazine. https://www.inc.com/minda-zetlin/how-the-most-effective-leaders-turn-weaknesses-into-strengths.html

19. Kabir, Homaira. n.d. "How to Let Go of Shoulds and Live by Your Musts." Happify. Accessed November 6, 2022. https://www.happify.com/hd/let-go-of-shoulds-and-live-by-your-musts/

20. Clear, James. n.d. "Let Your Values Drive Your Choices." James Clear. Accessed October 27, 2022. https://jamesclear.com/values-choices

21. Ward, Jenna. n.d. "How To Feel Your Body's Yes/No." Jenna Ward. Accessed October 27, 2022. https://jennaward.co/yes/

22. Ishak, Raven, Polish, Jay. 2017. "14 Signs Your Intuition Is Trying To Tell You Something — & How To Listen." Bustle. https://www.bustle.com/wellness/ways-to-know-if-your-intuition-is-trying-to-tell-you-something-how-to-listen-38787

23. BBC News. 2014. "Natan Sharansky: How chess kept one man sane." https://www.bbc.com/news/magazine-25560162

24. Adams, AJ. 2009. "Seeing Is Believing: The Power of Visualization." Psychology Today. https://www.psychologytoday.com/za/blog/flourish/200912/seeing-is-believing-the-power-visualization

25. Lohr, Jim. 2015. "Can Visualizing Your Body Doing Something Help You Learn to Do It Better?" Scientific American. https://www.

scientificamerican.com/article/can-visualizing-your-body-doing-something-help-you-learn-to-do-it-better/

26. University of Rochester Medical Center. n.d. "Journaling for Mental Health: Health Encyclopedia." Accessed October 27, 2022. https://www.urmc.rochester.edu/encyclopedia/content.aspx?ContentID=4552&ContentTypeID=1

27. Funk, Christine. 2015. "Maximize Your Strengths and Become Your Own Superhero." Bookboon. https://bookboon.com/blog/2015/11/be-your-own-superhero-maximize-your-strengths/

28. Locke, Robert. n.d. "The Stories Of These 5 Athletes Will Motivate Everyone Of You." Lifehack. Accessed September 30, 2022. https://www.lifehack.org/articles/communication/the-stories-these-5-athletes-will-motivate-everyone-you.html

29. Zvi. 2017. "Complexity Is Bad." Less Wrong. Accessed November 3, 2022. https://www.lesswrong.com/posts/WCxvmTyv9zYBPxTYJ/complexity-is-bad/

30. Morin, Amy. 2018. "5 Ways to Simplify Your Life." Psychology Today. https://www.psychologytoday.com/za/blog/what-mentally-strong-people-dont-do/201807/5-ways-simplify-your-life/

31. Phillips, Dawa Tarchin. 2016. "How to Curb Self-Defeating Habits." Mindful. https://www.mindful.org/curb-self-defeating-habits/

32. Avey, J. B., Wernsing, T. S., & Luthans, F. (2008). Can Positive Employees Help Positive Organizational Change? Impact of Psychological Capital and Emotions on Relevant Attitudes and Behaviors. The Journal of Applied Behavioral Science, 44(1), 48–70. https://doi.org/10.1177/0021886307311470

33. Solari, Nancy. n.d. "How To Let Go of Fear And Become Unstoppable." Lifehack. Accessed September 30, 2022. https://www.lifehack.org/891322/let-go-of-fear

34. NHS Inform. 2021. "Ten ways to fight your fears." Accessed October 27, 2022. https://www.nhsinform.scot/healthy-living/mental-wellbeing/fears-and-phobias/ten-ways-to-fight-your-fears

35. Dietz, Meredith. 2022. "How 'Negative Visualization' Can Make You More Positive." LifeHacker. https://lifehacker.com/how-negative-visualization-can-make-you-more-positive-1848462733/

36. DiGiulio, Sarah. 2018. "How to spot (and deal with) an energy vampire." NBC News. https://www.nbcnews.com/better/health/how-spot-deal-energy-vampire-ncna896251

37. Beeslaar, Eleanor. 2019. "Healthy vs. Unhealthy Boundaries." Healthy Relationships Initiative. https://healthyrelationshipsinitiative.org/healthy-vs-unhealthy-boundaries/

38. Delaware Psychological Services. 2020. "7 Ways to Remove Toxic People From Your Life." Accessed October 27, 2022. https://www.delawarepsychologicalservices.com/post/7-ways-to-remove-toxic-people-from-your-life

39. Tjan, Anthony K. 2015. "5 Ways to Become More Self-Aware." Harvard Business Review. https://hbr.org/2015/02/5-ways-to-become-more-self-aware

40. McRae, Lauren. 2019. "How to Start a New Routine and Stick To It." NorthShore University HealthSystem. https://www.northshore.org/healthy-you/how-to-start-a-new-routine-and-stick-to-it/

41. Gutierrez, Rebecca. n.d. "5 Key Elements to a Healthy Lifestyle--Renew by AdvoCare." AdvoCare® Connect. Accessed October 27,

2022. https://connect.advocare.com/5-key-elements-healthy-lifestyle/

42. The University of Toledo. n.d. "Self-Care: Counseling Center." Accessed October 27, 2022. https://www.utoledo.edu/studentaffairs/counseling/selfhelp/copingskills/selfcare.html

43. Choosing Therapy. 2021. "11 Ways to Practice Emotional Self Care." Accessed October 27, 2022. https://www.choosingtherapy.com/emotional-self-care/

44. Iowa AEA Mental Health. n.d. "Strategies for Social Self-Care." Accessed October 27, 2022. https://iowaaeamentalhealth.org/self-care/strategies-for-social-self-care/

45. Minimalism Made Simple. n.d. "How to Find Balance in Life (In 7 Easy Steps)." Accessed October 27, 2022. https://www.minimalismmadesimple.com/home/balance-in-life/

46. Steenbarger, Brett. 2021. "Three Keys To Making Life Changes." Forbes. https://www.forbes.com/sites/brettsteenbarger/2021/09/29/three-keys-to-making-life-changes/

47. Davis, Jeffrey. 2020. "4 Tips to Effectively Ask for Help—and Get a Yes." Psychology Today. https://www.psychologytoday.com/za/blog/tracking-wonder/202002/4-tips-effectively-ask-help-and-get-yes

48. Silvestre, Dan. 2017. "Personal Growth Plan: How to Write the Best One That Will Improve Life Dan Silvestre." Dan Silvestre. https://dansilvestre.com/personal-growth-plan/

49. Locke, Robert. n.d. "The Stories Of These 5 Athletes Will Motivate Everyone Of You." Lifehack. Accessed September 30, 2022. https://www.lifehack.org/articles/communication/the-stories-these-5-athletes-will-motivate-everyone-you.html

50. Mayo Clinic. 2022. "Self-esteem: Take steps to feel better about yourself." Accessed October 27, 2022. https://www.mayoclinic.org/healthy-lifestyle/adult-health/in-depth/self-esteem/art-20047976

51. National Health Service. n.d. "Raising low self-esteem." Accessed October 27, 2022. https://www.nhs.uk/mental-health/self-help/tips-and-support/raise-low-self-esteem/

52. Robbins, Kyle. n.d. "15 Simple Traits Of A Truly Good Person." Lifehack. Accessed October 27, 2022. https://www.lifehack.org/articles/communication/15-simple-traits-truly-good-person.html

53. Downey, Cheyenne. "How to Spot the Bad (and Good) People in Your Life." SpunOut. Accessed November 3, 2022. https://spunout.ie/voices/advice/spot-bad-good-people-in-life

54. Kirk, Melissa, Vinoth Chandar, and Joshua Denney. n.d. "5 Ways to Find Your People (The Ones Who Really Get You)." Tiny Buddha. Accessed October 27, 2022. https://tinybuddha.com/blog/5-ways-find-your-people-the-ones-who-really-get-you/

55. ReachOut Australia. n.d. "Decision making 101: Problem solving." Accessed October 27, 2022. https://au.reachout.com/articles/decision-making-101

56. Cook, Jodie. 2021. "Fix Your Keystone Habits To Transform Your Life." Forbes. https://www.forbes.com/sites/jodiecook/2021/01/11/fix-your-keystone-habits-to-transform-your-life/

57. True Citrus. 2018. "A Simple Way to Create New Habits: Use the Three." Accessed October 27, 2022. https://www.truelemon.com/blogs/tc/simple-way-create-new-habits

58. Bridges, Frances. 2019. "Five Ways To Make A Habit Stick." Forbes. https://www.forbes.com/sites/francesbridges/2019/02/25/five-ways-to-make-a-habit-stick/

59. Locke, Robert. n.d. "The Stories Of These 5 Athletes Will Motivate Everyone Of You." Lifehack. Accessed September 30, 2022. https://www.lifehack.org/articles/communication/the-stories-these-5-athletes-will-motivate-everyone-you.html

60. Barbash, Elyssa. 2017. "Perspective: The Difference Maker in Memories & Experiences." Psychology Today. https://www.psychologytoday.com/us/blog/trauma-and-hope/201704/perspective-the-difference-maker-in-memories-experiences

61. Schenck, Laura K. n.d. "How to Develop Mindfulness." Mindfulness Muse. Accessed October 27, 2022. https://www.mindfulnessmuse.com/mindfulness-exercises/how-to-develop-mindfulness

62. "Mindfulness exercises." n.d. Mayo Clinic. Accessed October 27, 2022. https://www.mayoclinic.org/healthy-lifestyle/consumer-health/in-depth/mindfulness-exercises/art-20046356

63. Scott, Elizabeth. 2022. "The Toxic Effects of Negative Self-Talk." Verywell Mind. https://www.verywellmind.com/negative-self-talk-and-how-it-affects-us-4161304

64. Shine. n.d. "How to Spot and Swap the 4 Types of Negative Self-Talk." Accessed October 27, 2022. https://advice.theshineapp.com/articles/how-to-spot-and-swap-the-4-types-of-negative-self-talk/

65. Cuncic, Arlin. 2021. "How Do You Live in the Present?" Verywell Mind. https://www.verywellmind.com/how-do-you-live-in-the-present-5204439

66. Borges, Anna. 2020. "9 Therapist-Approved Tips for Reframing Your Existential Anxiety." https://www.self.com/story/reframing-existential-anxiety/

67. Sutton, Jeremy. 2020. "Socratic Questioning in Psychology: Examples and Techniques." PositivePsychology.com. https://positivepsychology.com/socratic-questioning/

68. Harris, Sara. n.d. "Reframing Our Thoughts to Have Positive Feelings." AllHealth Network. Accessed October 27, 2022. https://www.allhealthnetwork.org/colorado-spirit/reframing-our-thoughts-to-have-positive-feelings/

69. Chauncey, Sarah. 2017. "Learning How to Observe Thoughts." Living the Mess. https://www.livingthemess.com/learning-observe-thoughts/

70. Mindful Staff. n.d. "How to Meditate." Mindful. Accessed October 27, 2022. https://www.mindful.org/how-to-meditate/

71. Indeed. 2021. "10 Focus Exercises To Help Improve Concentration Skills." Accessed October 27, 2022. https://www.indeed.com/career-advice/career-development/focus-exercises

72. Pullein, Carl. 2022. "How to Stop Multitasking and Become Way More Productive." Lifehack. https://www.lifehack.org/792689/how-to-stop-multitasking

73. Rhodes Sites. n.d. "Productivity: The Time Chunking Method." Accessed October 27, 2022. https://sites.rhodes.edu/academic-and-learning-resources/news/productivity-time-chunking-method

74. Dandapani. "Developing Willpower." Dandapani, February 27, 2019. https://dandapani.org/blog/developing-willpower/

75. Inspiring Tips. 2022. "Give Yourself Something To Look Forward To Every Day Challenge." Accessed October 27, 2022. https://inspiringtips.com/something-to-look-forward-to-challenge/

76. Rosen, Bob, and George Washington. 2018. "How to Find Your Higher Purpose." Psychology Today. https://www.psychologytoday.

com/za/blog/are-you-aware/201812/how-find-your-higher-purpose

77. Locke, Robert. n.d. "The Stories Of These 5 Athletes Will Motivate Everyone Of You." Lifehack. Accessed September 30, 2022. https://www.lifehack.org/articles/communication/the-stories-these-5-athletes-will-motivate-everyone-you.html

78. iMotions. 2015. "What Are Emotions and Why Do They Matter?" Accessed October 27, 2022. https://imotions.com/blog/emotions-matter/

79. Elmer, Jamie. 2022. "Why You Might Feel Like the Most Emotional Person in the Room." Healthline. Healthline Media. https://www.healthline.com/health/why-am-i-so-emotional-2

80. Cherry, Kendra. 2022. "Why Are Emotions Important?" Verywell Mind. https://www.verywellmind.com/the-purpose-of-emotions-2795181

81. Firestone, Lisa. 2018. "How Emotions Guide Our Lives." Psychology Today. https://www.psychologytoday.com/us/blog/compassion-matters/201801/how-emotions-guide-our-lives

82. Whitbourne, Susan K. 2021. "Your Most Important Emotional Tools." Psychology Today. https://www.psychologytoday.com/za/blog/fulfillment-any-age/202111/your-most-important-emotional-tools

83. Buckloh, Lisa M. n.d. "5 Ways to Know Your Feelings Better (for Teens)." Kids Health. Accessed October 27, 2022. https://kidshealth.org/en/teens/emotional-awareness.html

84. Gepp, Karin, and Nicole Washington. n.d. "How to Calm Down: 22 Things to Do When You're Anxious or Angry." Healthline. Accessed

October 27, 2022. https://www.healthline.com/health/how-to-calm-down

85. Bastos, Filipe. 2021. "Respond, Don't React: Taming Stress Through Mindful Presence--MindOwl." Mindowl. https://mindowl.org/respond-dont-react/

86. White, Marney A., and Karin Gepp. n.d. "Understanding Emotions: Connecting How you Feel with What it Means." Psych Central. Accessed October 27, 2022. https://psychcentral.com/health/understanding-what-your-emotions-are-trying-to-tell-you

87. Litner, Jennifer, Maya Chastain, and Joslyn Jelinek. 2021. "Where Emotions Get Trapped In The Body and How to Release Them." Healthline. https://www.healthline.com/health/mind-body/how-to-release-emotional-baggage-and-the-tension-that-goes-with-it

88. Handel, Steven. n.d. "50 Ways To Constructively Channel Negative Emotions." The Emotion Machine. Accessed October 27, 2022. https://www.theemotionmachine.com/50-ways-to-constructively-channel-negative-emotions/

89. HelpGuide.org. n.d. "Emotional Intelligence Toolkit." Accessed October 27, 2022. https://www.helpguide.org/articles/mental-health/emotional-intelligence-toolkit.htm

90. Conn, Chris. n.d. "10 Amazing Sports Stories That Should Be Made into Movies." Bleacher Report. Accessed October 27, 2022. https://bleacherreport.com/articles/770621-10-amazing-sports-stories-that-should-be-made-into-movies

91. Miller, Therese, and Richard C. Bell. 2008. "Sport and Spirituality: A Comparative Perspective – The Sport Journal." The Sport Journal. https://thesportjournal.org/article/sport-and-spirituality-a-comparative-perspective/

92. Katz, Ali. 2014. "6 Steps To Invite Spirituality Into Your Life Every Day." MindBodyGreen. https://www.mindbodygreen.com/0-16223/6-steps-to-invite-spirituality-into-your-life-every-day.html

93. Ho, Leon. 2022. "What Is the Meaning of Life? A Guide to Living a Meaningful Life." Lifehack. https://www.lifehack.org/articles/communication/how-put-meaning-back-into-your-life.html

94. Israel, Ira. n.d. "3 Ways to Find Meaning in Life." wikiHow. Accessed October 27, 2022. https://www.wikihow.com/Find-Meaning-in-Life/

95. Delagran, Louise. n.d. "How Does Nature Impact Our Wellbeing?" Taking Charge of Your Health & Wellbeing. Accessed November 11, 2022. https://www.takingcharge.csh.umn.edu/how-does-nature-impact-our-wellbeing#:~:text=Exposure%20to%20nature%20not%20only,health%20researchers%20Stamatakis%20and%20Mitchell

96. Castellani, Robyn. 2018. "Want To Change Your Life? Change Your Narrative. Here's How." Forbes. https://www.forbes.com/sites/break-the-future/2018/07/17/want-to-change-your-life-change-your-narrative-heres-how/

97. Carpenter, Derrick. n.d. "The Science Behind Gratitude (and How It Can Change Your Life). Accessed October 27, 2022. https://www.happify.com/hd/the-science-behind-gratitude/

98. Mindful Staff. 2022. "How to Practice Gratitude." Mindful. Accessed October 27, 2022. https://www.mindful.org/how-to-practice-gratitude/

99. Nazish, Noma. 2018. "Five Science-Backed Ways To Practice Gratitude Every Day." Forbes. https://www.forbes.com/sites/nomanazish/2018/11/21/five-science-backed-ways-to-practice-gratitude-every-day/

100. Becker, Joshua. n.d. "The 10 Most Important Things to Simplify in Your Life." Becoming Minimalist. Accessed October 27, 2022. https://www.becomingminimalist.com/the-10-most-important-things-to-simplify-in-your-life/

101. Morin, Amy. 2018. "5 Ways to Simplify Your Life." Psychology Today. https://www.psychologytoday.com/za/blog/what-mentally-strong-people-dont-do/201807/5-ways-simplify-your-life

102. Garrett, Michelle. n.d. "Creating Your Personal Motto." Divas with a Purpose. Accessed October 27, 2022. https://www.divaswithapurpose.com/creating-personal-motto/

103. Kristenson, Sarah. 2021. "81 Personal Mottos Ideas & Examples to Live By." Happier Human. https://www.happierhuman.com/personal-motto/

104. Sharma, Sunil. 2019. "Phil Jackson the Zen Master who conquered basketball." Sunil Sharma. https://sunilsharmauk.medium.com/phil-jackson-the-zen-master-who-conquered-basketball-e8257a76979d

105. Crossley, Tracy. 2018. "Journey of Attachment: Resistance to Reality." Tracy Crossley. https://tracycrossley.com/217-journey-attachment-resistance-reality/

106. Seltzer, Leon F. 2016. "You Only Get More of What You Resist—Why?" Psychology Today. https://www.psychologytoday.com/us/blog/evolution-the-self/201606/you-only-get-more-what-you-resist-why

107. Babauta, Leo. n.d. "12 Essential Rules to Live More Like a Zen Monk." Zen Habits. Accessed October 27, 2022. https://zenhabits.net/12-essential-rules-to-live-more-like-a-zen-monk/

108. David, Natalia S., and Deborah Ryan. n.d. "3 Ways to Practice Non Attachment." wikiHow. Accessed October 27, 2022. https://www.wikihow.com/Practice-Non-Attachment

109. ReGain Editorial Team. 2022. "What Is Non-Attachment, and How Can I Learn It?" Regain. https://www.regain.us/advice/attachment/what-is-non-attachment-and-how-can-i-learn-it/

110. Mayo Clinic. 2020. "Forgiveness: Letting go of grudges and bitterness." Accessed October 27, 2022. https://www.mayoclinic.org/healthy-lifestyle/adult-health/in-depth/forgiveness/art-20047692

111. Griffey, Harriet. n.d. "5 tips to help you let go of the past and move on." Calm Moment. Accessed October 27, 2022. https://www.calmmoment.com/wellbeing/how-to-learn-the-lessons-of-the-past-and-let-them-go/

112. Robyn, Fiona. 2018. "Difficult Lessons: How to Learn What You Need to and Move On." Tiny Buddha. https://tinybuddha.com/blog/difficult-lessons-how-to-learn-what-you-need-to-and-move-on/

113. Legg, Timothy J. n.d. "How to Stop Ruminating: 10 Tips to Stop Repetitive Thoughts." Healthline. Accessed October 27, 2022. https://www.healthline.com/health/how-to-stop-ruminating

114. Compitus, Katherine, and William Smith. 2020. "12 Radical Acceptance Worksheets For Your DBT Sessions." PositivePsychology.com. https://positivepsychology.com/radical-acceptance-worksheets/

115. Trotter, Jake, and ESPN Staff. 2017. "From 7th-grade phenom to failed QB to elite receiver." ESPN. https://africa.espn.com/college-

football/story/_/id/20923614/west-virginia-david-sills-7th-grade-phenom-failed-qb-elite-receiver

116. Harrison, Melinda. n.d. "What Parents of Teen Athletes Need to Know about Life After Sports—Your Teen Mag." Your Teen Magazine. Accessed October 27, 2022. https://yourteenmag.com/sports/life-after-sports-teen-athletes

117. Bleacher Report. n.d. "12 Insane Youth Sports Stories: News, Scores, Highlights, Stats, and Rumors." Accessed October 27, 2022. https://bleacherreport.com/articles/1697114-12-insane-youth-sports-stories

www.ingramcontent.com/pod-product-compliance
Lightning Source LLC
Chambersburg PA
CBHW050855150626
46549CB00013B/2165